SHAANXI HISTORY MUSEUM

Editor-in-Chief:Feng Gengwu

Edited by Shaanxi History Museum

Shaanxi Tourism Publishing House

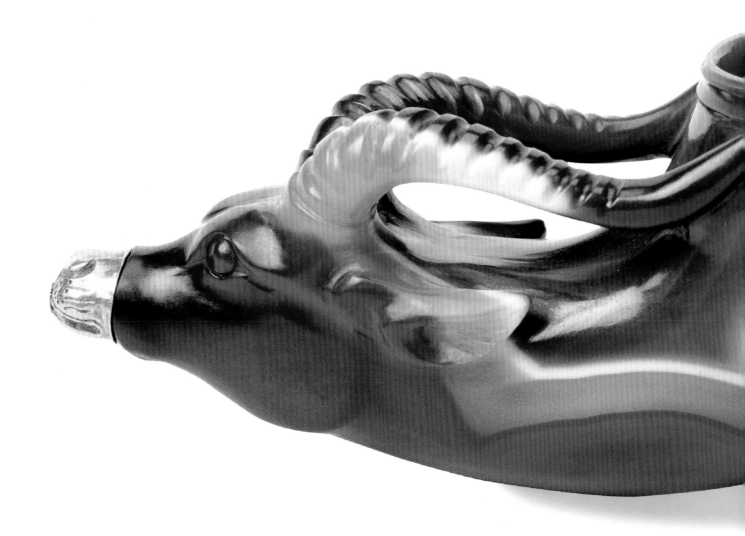

Beast-head-shaped agate cup,a wine vessel

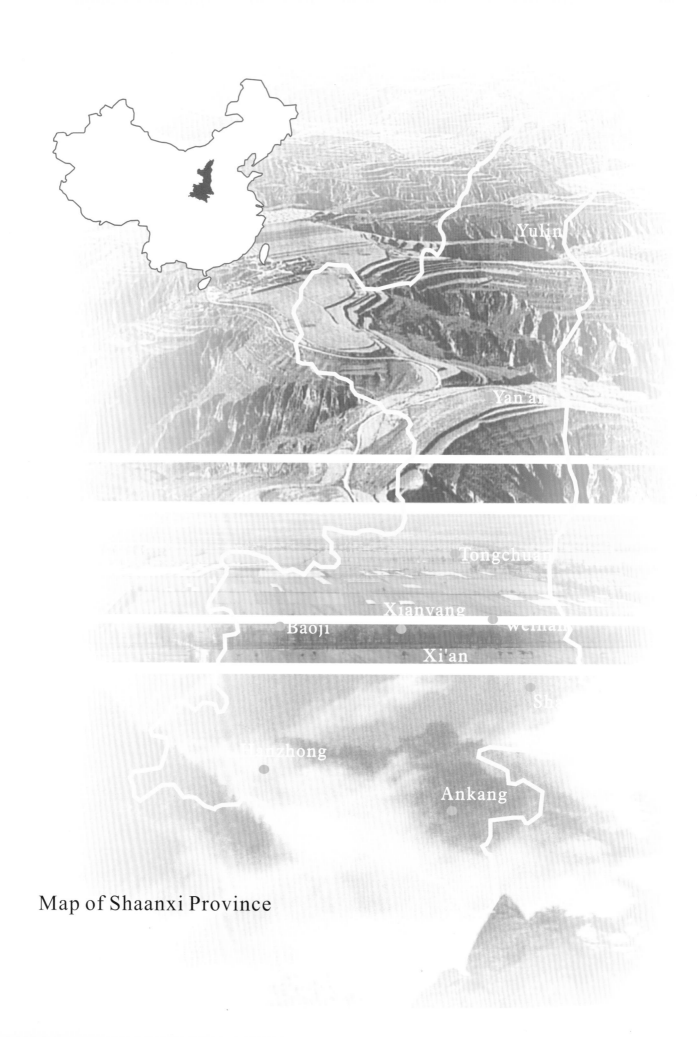

Yulin

Yan'an

Tongchuan

Xianyang

Baoji   Weinan

Xi'an

Sh

Hanzhong

Ankang

Map of Shaanxi Province

Contents

1. Foreword 2

2. Introduction 4

    (1) Location Map of Shaanxi History Museum in Xi'an 8

    (2) Map of Shaanxi History Museum and Environs 9

    (3) View of Shaanxi History Museum 10

    (4) View of the Opening Ceremony of Shaanxi History Museum 12

3. The Buildings 14

    (1) Map Showing the Functions of the Buildings 20

    (2) Diagram of the Visitor's Route 21

4. Exhibitions 22

    (1) The Main Exhibition 24

    (2) The Monograph Exhibitions 32

    (3) The Temporary Exhibitions 34

    (4) Exhibitions Held Abroad 36

5. Exceptional Cultural Relics 38

    (1) The National Treasures 39

    (2) Selected Cultural Relics 50

          Bronzes(50); Gold and silver wares(66); Frescoes(80); Pottery figurines(94); Pottery and porcelains(116); Bricks and tile-ends(126); Bronze mirrors(134); Jade wares(147); Coins(154); Other(160)

FOREWORD

The Three-Qin Area (also called Shaanxi Province) is one of the important regions in which Chinese civilisation was born and developed. Also, 13 prosperous dynasties, including the Zhou, Qin, Han and Tang, built their capitals here. Abundant historic remains show the unique cultural styles and features of Shaanxi. Enjoying the reputation of being 'a bright pearl in an ancient city' and 'a treasure house of China', Shaanxi History Museum is a showhouse of art from Shaanxi history and ancient Chinese civilisation.

Shaanxi History Museum is located to the north-west of the Big Goose Pagoda. The planning for its establishment started in 1983 and construction was completed on June 20th, 1991. As the first national museum equipped with modern facilities, it is a milestone symbolising the new development of museums in China.

The Museum consists of a group of buildings of Tang Dynasty architectural style, including palace-styled halls in the centre and elegant pavilions in the four corners. Representing the traditional Chinese aesthetic principle of 'perfect symmetry with a central-axle line', its layout is perfectly ordered. The whole structure appears elegant and dignified, and is an excellent combination of national traditions, local features and the spirit of the times. The Museum covers about 65,000 square metres with the buildings covering 55,600 square meters. The storehouses occupy 8,000 square metres and the exhibition halls some 11,000 square metres. The cultural relics collected here number more than 370,000 pieces, originating from one million years ago up to 1840 AD in the Qing Dynasty. With large quantities and varieties of importance and great value, the collection is outstanding, including such treasures as: the exquisite bronzes of the Shang and Zhou Dynasties, the vivid pottery figurines of successive dynasties, the well-known gold and silver wares of the Han and Tang Dynasties and the matchless Tang Tomb frescoes.

Shaanxi History Museum is a comprehensive history museum. Since it opened to the public, it has made full use of its advantages, primarily that it possesses exquisite historic relics in complete groups. Keeping to the principle of 'protecting effectively, utilising rationally and managing conscientiously', the Museum has been holding cultural relices exhibitions in various forms. Integrating 'collection, education, protection, scientific research and publicity', it has set up a display system that consists of three related exhibitions: the Main Exhibition, the Monograph Exhibition and the Temporary Exhibition.

The Museum shows the profound and extensive cultural achievements of ancient China. With its excellent displays, elegant surroundings and unique character, the Museum attracts large numbers of visitors from China and overseas. It has become an important place for publicising the rich culture of China as well as conducting external exchanges. In the 21st century, Shaanxi History Museum promises to continue to contribute even more with its new and exciting outlook.

INTRODUCTION

Occupying a total area of 205,603 square kilometres, Shaanxi is situated in the central part of China; 32' 42" to 39' 35" latitude north and 105' 29" to 111' 15" longitude east. Shaanxi is composed of three parts: the Loess Plateau in northern Shaanxi, the mountainous region of the Qinling Mountains, Daba Mountain and the valley of the Hanshui River in southern Shaanxi, and the alluvial plain of the Weihe River in central Shaanxi. The Weihe River Plain is a long, narrow, low-lying basin with an average elevation of 500 metres, some 300 kilometres long; it is known as the 'Qin Plain of 800 Li'. (Li is a Chinese unit of measurement equivalent to about half a kilometre.) Shaanxi lies on a transitional area between humid south-east China and arid north-west China; it can be divided into three basic regions: a mid temperate zone, a southern temperate zone and a northern subtropical zone.

Since ancient times the Weihe River Plain has been one of the main agricultural regions of China. Around it there are four strategic passes: the Hangu Pass to the east, the Wuguan Pass to the south, the Sanguan Pass to the west and the Xiaoguan Pass to the north. These passes made the Plain an ideal strategic location during ancient wars.

Xi'an is situated in the centre of the Weihe River Plain and its climate is mild and humid, with an average temperature of 13.3℃ and an annual rainfall of 604mm. This climate is excellent for growing plants and makes a pleasant area in which to live. The primitive peoples of the Palaeolithic Age lived in this area as early as 1 million years ago. Evidence for this includes the skull fossil of the 'Lantian Ape' found at Gongwangling in Lantian County, about 50 kilometres south-east of Xi'an. Around Xi'an, village sites from the Neolithic Age were also found; these include the Banpo Site which is about 6,000 years old and the Jiangzhai Site which is between 5,000-6,000 years old.

In China's history there are 14 dynasties or kingdoms, lasting some 1,077 years, that built their capitals in Shaanxi. Among them, 13 dynasties chose Xi'an and its surroundings as their capitals; this lasted for 1,053 years. They include the following:

In the 11 century BC, Wuwang of the Zhou Dynasty built his capital, Haojing, on the banks of the Fenghe River just to the west of Xi'an. Haojing remained the capital for about 300 years.

Between 221 and 207 BC, Qinshihuang, the first Emperor of China, built the Qin Dynasty capital at Xianyang.

Between 206 BC and 8 AD, the Western Han Dynasty built its capital at Xi'an, and named it Chang'an, meaning 'being peaceful forever'.

Between 9 and 24 AD, Wangmang situated the Xin Dynasty capital in Chang'an.

Between 190 and 195 AD, Emperor Xiandi of the Eastern Han Dynasty moved his capital to Chang'an.

Between 313 and 316 AD, Chang'an was the capital of the Western Jin Dynasty.

Between 319 and 329 AD, Liu Yao situated the Qian Zhao Kingdom capital in Chang'an.

Between 351 and 383 AD, Fu Jian situated the Qian Qin Kingdom capital in Chang'an.

Between 384 and 417 AD, Yao Chang built the Hou Qin Kingdom capital in Chang'an.

Between 407 and 431 AD, the Da Xia Kingdom made Tongwan City (today's Baichengzi in Jingbian County, northern Shaanxi) its capital.

Between 535 and 557 AD, the Western Wei Dynasty made Chang'an its capital.

Between 557 and 581 AD, Chang'an was the capital of the Northern Zhou Dynasty.

Between 581 and 618 AD, Yangjian situated the Sui Dynasty capital in Chang'an; he rebuilt it and changed its name to 'Da Xing City'.

Between 618 and 907 AD, the Tang Dynasty capital was built by Li Yuan at Chang'an and lasted for 289 years.

After the Tang Dynasty, the centres of politics, economics and culture gradually moved eastward and southward. The Shaanxi area fell into decline, although it was still regarded as an important cultural centre within China. As one of the famous 'six ancient capitals' and the starting point of the Silk Road, Xi'an and its surrounding districts possess many cultural remains from different eras. The tomb of the first Chinese Emperor, the tombs of 11 of the Western Han Dynasty Emperors, and 18 Emperor's tombs from the Tang Dynasty, are all found in Shaanxi Province. Furthermore, other nations also left their historical remains here as a result of ancient cultural and economic exchanges.

Shaanxi occupies a special position in China's history. Since the methods of modern archaeology spread throughout China, researchers have made discoveries here many times. In the early 1920's, Frenchmen Emile Licent and Pierre Teihard de Chardin, excavated in Hetao Area of the Huanghe River. Between 1933 and 1935, two Chinese men, Xu Xusheng and Su Bingqi, excavated sites in Baoji, Fengxiang and Chang'an; they found many artifacts and this was regarded as the real starting point of modern archaeological research in Shaanxi. Ever since the 1950's, important archaeological finds have been made here. These include the discovery of the fossil of 'Lantian Ape' in Lantian County, the Banpo Village Site, the excavation of 103 bronzes of the Wei Family in Fufeng County, the discovery of the sarira of Buddha and some royal treasures from the crypt of the Famen Temple in Fufeng County, the unearthing of the Tang Tombs of the nobles and their frescoes, the discovery of the Terra-cotta Warriors and Horses of Emperor Qinshihuang.

All of these discoveries illustrate features of ancient history and culture in a remarkable way. They show that, from remote antiquity to the late 19th Century, Shaanxi was constantly at the forefront of production, culture and customs. They also show that historic remains, from various eras, are dispersed extensively from north to south within Shaanxi, and confirm that the cultural relics of Shaanxi form a unique historic system for research.

In the Shaanxi History Museum, the superb collection of unique exhibits enable visitors to understand and enjoy the amazing times that existed here thousands of years ago.

CHINESE CHRONOLOGY

The Paleolithic Age	Circa 1,000,000 --- 10,000 years ago
The Neolithic Age	Circa 10,000 --- 4,000 years ago
The Xia Dynasty	Circa 22nd --- 17th century BC
The Shang Dynasty	Circa 17th --- 11th century BC
The Western Zhou Dynasty	Circa 11th century --- 771 BC
The Spring and Autumn Period	771 --- 475 BC
The Warring States Period	475 --- 221 BC
The Qin Dynasty	221 --- 206 BC
The Han Dynasty	206 BC --- 220 AD
The Three Kingdoms	220 --- 280 AD
The Jin Dynasty	265 ---420 AD
The Southern and Northern Dynasties	420 --- 589 AD
The Southern Dynasties: Song	420 --- 479 AD
Qi	479 ---502 AD
Liang	502 ---557 AD

		Chen	557 --- 589 AD
The Northern Dynasties:	Northern Wei		386 --- 534 AD
	Eastern Wei		534 --- 550 AD
	Western Wei		535 --- 556 AD
	Northern Qi		550 --- 577 AD
	Northern Zhou		557 --- 581 AD
The Sui Dynasty			581 --- 618 AD
The Tang Dynasty			618 --- 907 AD
The Five Dynasties			907 --- 960 AD
The Song Dynasty			960 --- 1279 AD
The Liao Kingdom			916 --- 1125 AD
The Jin Kingdom			1115 --- 1234 AD
The Yuan Dynasty			1271 --- 1368 AD
The Ming Dynasty			1368 --- 1644 AD
The Qing Dynasty			1644 --- 1911 AD

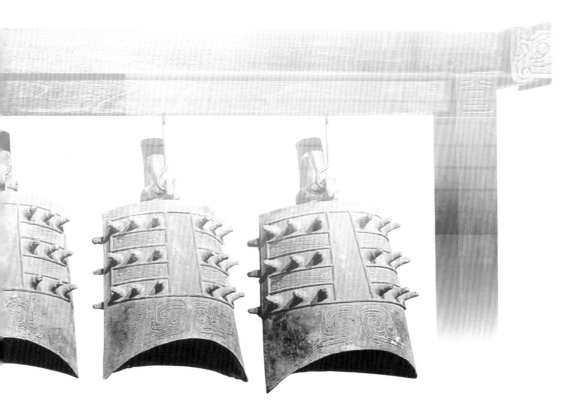

Location Map of Shaanxi History Museum in Xi'an

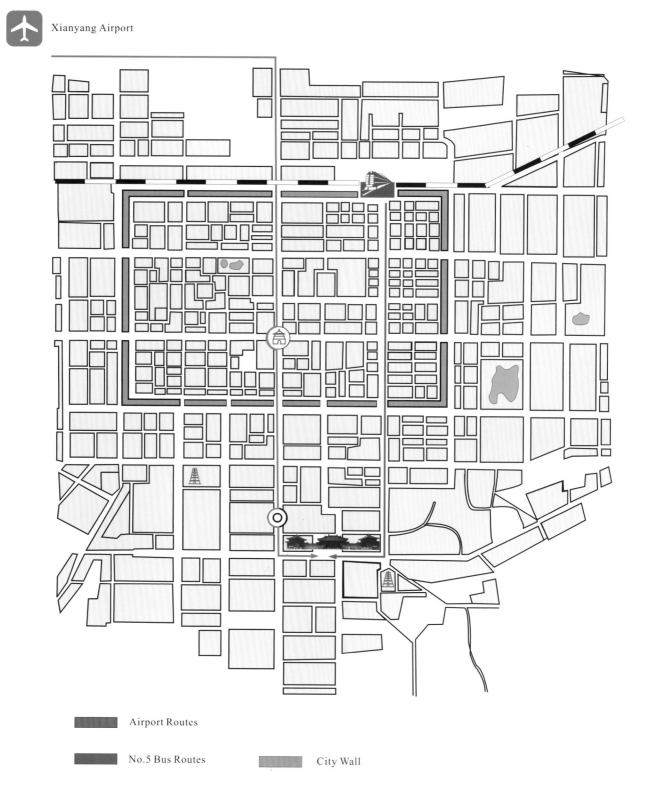

Xianyang Airport

Airport Routes

No.5 Bus Routes

City Wall

Map of Shaanxi History Museum and Environs

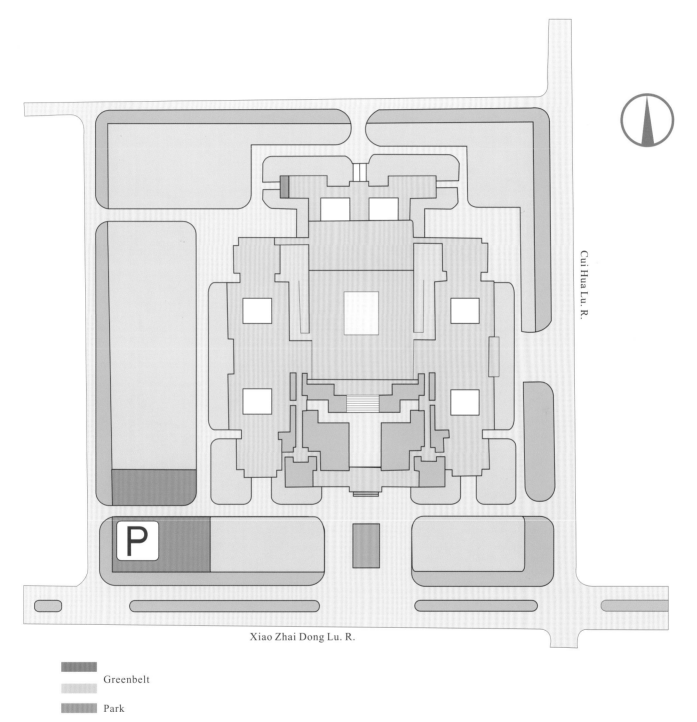

Cui Hua Lu. R.

Xiao Zhai Dong Lu. R.

Greenbelt

Park

Building

Road

Courtyard

Pool

View of Shaanxi History Museum

View of the Opening Ceremony of Shaanxi History Museum
(Photographed by Hua Xinmin)

Shaanxi History Museum was designed by a scholar of the China Engineering Academy and famous master of architectural design, Ms. Zhang Jinqiu. The structure was built in traditional Chinese architectural style, a layout of perfect symmetry and courtyard-styled buildings. The main building is located in the northern part and faces south. Along the central line there are arranged, the Main Entrance, the Front Courtyard, the Initial Hall, the Main Exhibition Hall and the Storehouse. In the east is the Temporary Exhibition Hall (also called the Eastern Exhibition Hall), and in the west, the Monograph Exhibition Hall. At the south-eastern, north-eastern, south-western and north-western corners of the Museum, lie four pavilions used as the Multi-Function Hall, the Stock & Reading Room, the Museum Shop and the Administration Office. With a combination of Tang-styled architecture and modern technology, the elegant and imposing Museum has become one of the important buildings to symbolise Xi'an and Shaanxi Province.

The Main Entrance

14

The Outside Scene of the Eastern Exhibition Hall
(Photographed by Liu Hexin)

The Northern Gate

Corner of the Front Courtyard

The Front Corridor of the Hall

The Main Exhibition Hall

The Winding Corridor of the Courtyard

The Profile of the Hall

Map Showing the Functions of the Buildings

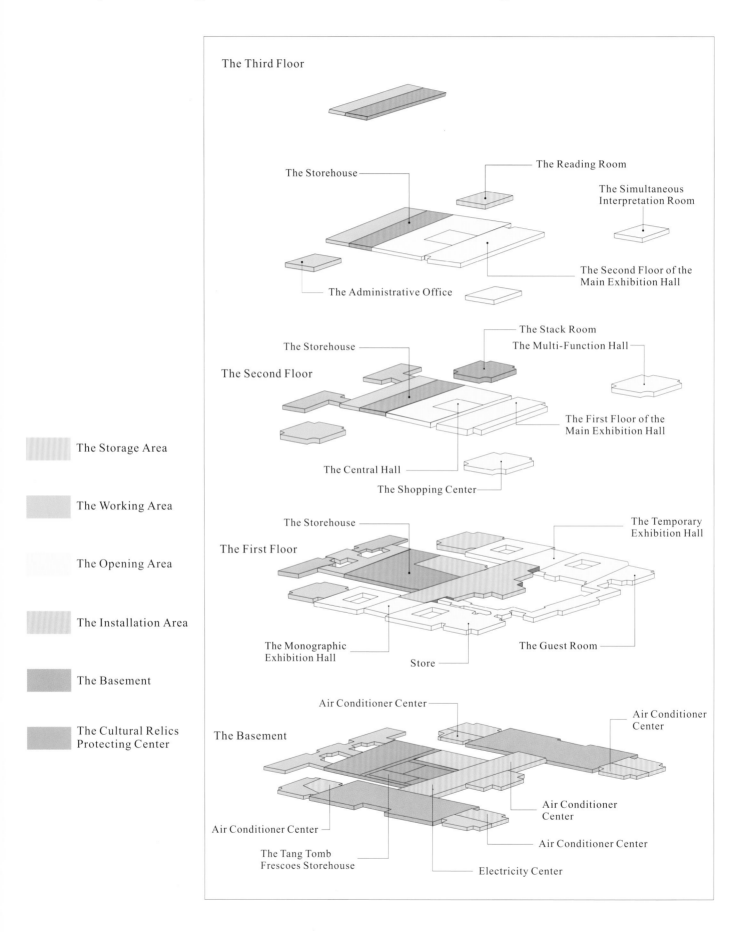

The Third Floor

The Storehouse

The Reading Room

The Simultaneous Interpretation Room

The Second Floor of the Main Exhibition Hall

The Administrative Office

The Stack Room
The Multi-Function Hall

The Storehouse

The Second Floor

The First Floor of the Main Exhibition Hall

The Central Hall

The Shopping Center

The Storehouse

The Temporary Exhibition Hall

The First Floor

The Monographic Exhibition Hall

Store

The Guest Room

Air Conditioner Center

Air Conditioner Center

The Basement

Air Conditioner Center

Air Conditioner Center

Air Conditioner Center

The Tang Tomb Frescoes Storehouse

Electricity Center

The Storage Area

The Working Area

The Opening Area

The Installation Area

The Basement

The Cultural Relics Protecting Center

Diagram of the Vistor's Route

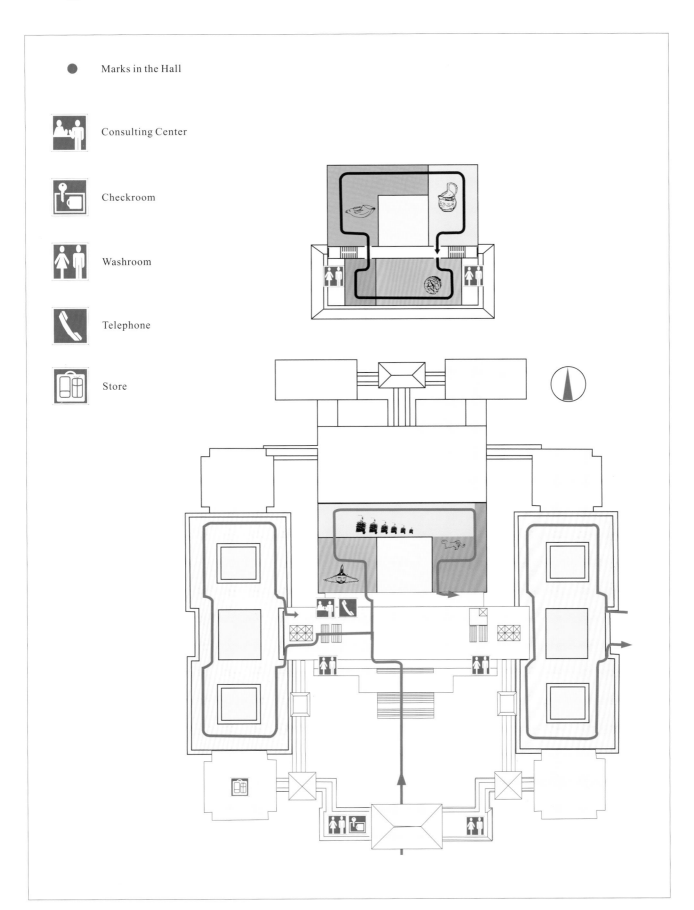

- ● Marks in the Hall
- Consulting Center
- Checkroom
- Washroom
- Telephone
- Store

The Shaanxi History Museum is a comprehensive museum. The whole area measures some 11,000 square metres and is divided into three parts: the Main Exhibition Hall, the Monograph Exhibition Hall and the Temporary Exhibition Hall.

The Initial Hall

The Main Exhibition Hall, in the centre of the Museum, covers an area of 6,000 square metres. 'The Exhibition of Shaanxi Ancient History' is the permanent exhibition held in the Museum. The history of Shaanxi has been divided into seven sections:

The Prehistoric Age
The Zhou Dynasty
The Qin Dynasty
The Han Dynasty
The Wei Dynasty to the Southern and Northern Dynasties
The Sui Dynasty to the Tang Dynasty
The Song Dynasty to the Qing Dynasty

From our collections, more than 2,000 pieces were chosen as representative of these eras. Laying emphasis on the Zhou, Qin, Han and Tang Dynasties, the main exhibition clearly shows the development of Shaanxi Province from the Lantian Ape to the time before the Opium War, a period of about one million years.

史前

The Prehistoric Age

周

The Zhou Dynasty

The Qin Dynasty

The Han Dynasty

汉

魏晋南北朝

The Wei Dynasty to
the Southern and Northern
Dynasties

隋唐

宋元明清

The Song Dynasty to
the Qing Dynasty

The total area of the Monograph Exhibition Hall, which is situated to the west of the Main Exhibition Hall, is about 2,500 square metres. It was used to show the monograph exhibitions. The exhibitions that have been held here include 'The Exhibition of the Shaanxi Bronze Treasures' and 'Exhibition of the Pottery Selects of Shaanxi Province in the Past Dynasties',etc.At present 'Exhibition of the Rare Gems of the New Archaeological Discoveries in Shaanxi' is being exhibited. This hall presents visitors with the new advances in research into cultural relics and archaeological excavations in Shaanxi Province.

The Museum is preparing to build the 'Tang Tomb Frescoes Exhibition Centre',with unique features embodying the protection, display and scientific research of the Tang Tomb Frescoes and showing a historical picture of Tang society.

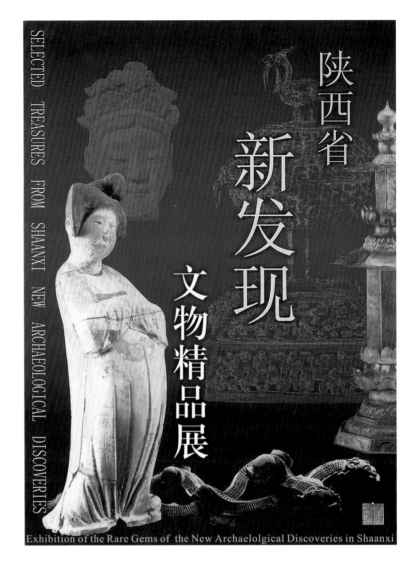

Exhibition of the Rare Gems of the New Archaelolgical Discoveries in Shaanxi

The Exhibition of the Shaanxi Bronze Treasures

Exhibition of the Pottery Selects of Shaanxi Province in the Past Dynasties

The Tang Tomb Frescoes Storehouse

33

Survey of the Eastern Exhibition Hall

Located to the east of the Main Exhibition Hall, the Eastern Exhibition Hall has a floor space of 2,500 square metres and several temporary exhibitions from China and other countries have been shown here. These include 'The Exhibition of Selected Cultural Relics from Zhaoling' , 'The Exhibition of the Original Murals from the Tang Mausoleums' , 'Exhibition of Cultural Relics from the Tomb of Princess Chenguo of the State of Liao' , 'The Exhibition of the Women's Dresses and Personal Adornments of the Tang Dynasty', 'Gold and Silver Treasures of Tang',etc. The abundant content, distinctive design and useful information included here help to produce an influential display system at home and abroad.

The Exhibition of Women's Dresses and Personal Adornments of the Tang Dynasty

Gold and Silver Treasures of Tang

The Capital Museum-Highlights of the Cultural Relics of Yuan, Ming and Qing Dynasties

Table of the Exhibitions Held Abroad

Time	Site	Name of Exhibition
1991.1—1992.11	Singapore	The Silk Road --- Treasures of Tang, China
1992.7—1992.11	Japan	The Capital of Silk Road --- Exhibition of the Treasures of Chang'an, China
1992.9—1992.11	Japan	The Frescoes Exhibition of the Tang Dynasty
1993.2—1993.3	France	Exhibition of the Tang Treasures
1993.9—1993.12	Germany	Chinas Goldenes Zeitalter - Die Tang Dynastie und das Kulturelle Erbe der Seidenstrasse
1993.10—1994.1	Hongkong	Treasures of Chang'an Capital of the Silk Road
1994.2—1994.3	Japan	Treasures of Chang'an and the Great Wall
1994.8—1995.6	USA	Tomb Treasures from China --- The Buried Art of Ancient Xi'an
1994.8—1995.9	South Korea	Exhibition of Emperor Qinshihuang
1994.9—1994.11	Japan	Exhibition of Chang'an, Capital of the Tang Dynasty
1994.9—1995.6	Japan	Emperor Qinshihuang and His Times
1995.4—1995.9	USA	Imperial Tombs of China
1996.3—1997.2	Japan	Women in Chang'an --- The Glory of the Tang Empire
1996.10—1996.11	Japan	Gold & Silver Treasures and Architectural Remains from Tang Dynasty in China
1997.2—1997.5	USA	Treasures from the First Emperor of China
1997.3—1997.6	Japan	Emperor Qinshihuang and Great Terra-Cotta Warriors and Horses
1997.6—1997.9	Finland	Emperor's Army
1997.9—1998.5	Japan	The First Emperor
1997.10—1998.5	Japan	The Masterpieces of Yaozhou Ware
1998.3—1998.10	USA	Eternal China: Splendors from Ancient Xi'an
1998.9—1998.11	South Korea	'98 Kyongju World Culture Expo --- Yellow River Civilization
1998.10—1999.8	Japan	The Glory of the Court --- Tang Dynasty Empress Wu and Her Times
1999.4—1999.11	Japan	Treasures of the Silk Road, China
1999.6—2000.6	Japan	Exhibition of Chinese Sculptures of Qin and Han Dynasties
1999.9—2000.7	Japan	Gifts of the Tang Emperors --- Hidden Treasures from the Famen Temple
1999.10—2000.2	UK	Gilded Dragons
2000.3—2000.11	Japan	Exhibition of the Terra-Cotta Warriors and Horses of the Qin Dynasty
2000.5—2000.8	USA	Imperial China: The Art of the Horses in Chinese History
2000.8—2001.6	Japan	Chinese Civilization Exhibition
2000.9—2001.4	Mexico	Imperial China: The Dynasties of Xi'an
2000.10—2000.12	Japan	Treasures of Ancient China
2000.11—2001.1	France	Exhibition of Chinese Archaeological Finds
2001.7—2001.8	Monaco	China: The First Emperor's Century

As a window for displaying the ancient civilisation of Shaanxi and China, the Shaanxi History Museum maintains close cultural exchanges with many famous museums, galleries, research institutes and colleges all over the world. Since the museum opened, more than 30 exhibitions have been held in Asia, Europe and America. The Museum contributes much and helps the world learn more about China.

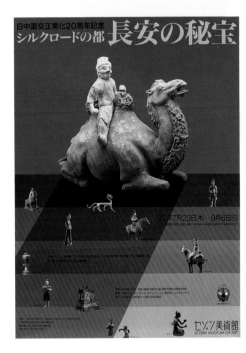

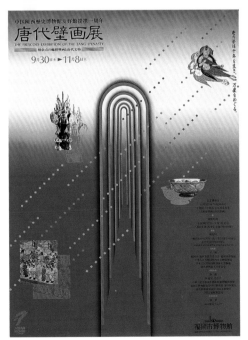

Exceptional Cultural Relics

The Shaanxi History Museum has collected more than 370,000 pieces, including 3,700 bronzes, 1,000 mirrors, 18,000 pieces of pottery, 2,000 pottery figurines, 1,700 gold and silver pieces, more than 1,000 square metres of Tang Tomb Frescoes, and a large number of coins, jade, calligraphy and painted scrolls. Among all of these, the pieces from the Zhou, Qin, Han and Tang Dynasties are particularly magnificent, representative and unique. According to national authentication, 18 pieces are among the most valuable national treasures in China and 765 groups are first-grade relics. The Museum's collection is amongst the best in China.

The Shaanxi History Museum has collected 18 groups of national treasures, consisting of gold and silver wares, bronzes, frescoes, porcelains, pottery figurines and jade wares. All of them are of great historic and artistic value.

Duo You Ding , A Tripod

Late Period of the Western Zhou Dynasty
Height: 51.5 cm   Diameter of Mouth: 50cm
Unearthed in 1980 from Xiaquan Village, Chang'an County, Shaanxi Province

As a ceremonial food vessel, this tripod was the most popular form of ancient Chinese bronze vessel. Inside it was inscribed with 278 characters, which were regarded as important material for researching the war history of the Western Zhou Dynasty and the relationship between the Zhou people and Yan Yun (a minority nationality in northern China) during the reign of King Li.

The Empress' Jade Seal Inscribed with Characters "Huang Hou Zhi Xi"

The Western Han Dynasty
Height: 2 cm   Side Length: 2.8 cm
Unearthed in 1968 at Liangjiagou, Xianyang, Shaanxi Province

   This seal was made of He Tian jade from Xinjiang Uygur Autonomous Region. With a monster-shaped protrusion as a knob, the seal was inscribed with 4 characters 'Huang Hou Zhi Xi' which means it is an empress' seal. It was unearthed just 1 km from Changling, the mausoleum of Emperor Gaozu (named Liu Bang) and his wife (named Lye Zhi). Therefore, it may have been used by Empress Lye Zhi. The jade seal is one of the most important seals which have ever been found.

Silver Pot with A Hoop Handle and Parrot Design

The Tang Dynasty
Height: 24.2 cm   Diameter of Mouth: 12.4 cm
Diameter of Base: 14.3cm
Unearthed in 1970 from Hejiacun, Xi'an

    This artifact was hammered into shape and engraved with parrot and flower designs on the pot, and grape, pomegranate and honeysuckle designs on the lid. Inside the lid there are two lines of characters 'Zi Ying Wu Shi Liang', 'Bai Ying Shi Er Liang' which were written in ink.

Beast-Head-Shaped Agate Cup, A Wine Vessel

The Tang Dynasty
Length: 15.5 cm   Diameter of Mouth: 5.9 cm
Unearthed in1970 at Hejiacun, Xi'an

With an exotic style, this cup was made in the shape of a beast's head. It has an antelope-head-shaped handle. If the gold on its mouth was removed, wine could flow out of the mouth. It was regarded as proof of the cultural exchange between China and other nations during the Tang Dynasty.

Gold Bowl with Mandarin Ducks and Lotus Petals Design

The Tang Dynasty
Height: 5.5 cm Diameter of Mouth: 13.7 cm Diameter of Base: 6.7 cm
Unearthed in 1970 at Hejiacun, Xi'an

    This bowl was hammered into shape. On the outside it is engraved with two layers of lotus petal designs, and each layer has ten petals. The upper layer was engraved with various animal designs: fox, rabbit, river deer, deer, parrot, Mandarin duck, flower and straw. The lower layer was decorated with honeysuckle. There is a rose carved on its inner base, and on its inner belly, there were three characters 'Jiu Liang Ban' written in ink.

Tri-Colored Camel Carrying A Group of Musicians

The Tang Dynasty
Height: 58 cm
Unearthed in 1959 in Zhongbucun, Xi'an

Between the camel's humps was laid an elliptical mat. A platform with a blanket on it was placed on the mat. Seven musicians carrying sheng, flute, pi ba, kong hou, clapper etc. sit on the blanket, with a singer standing in the center.

Playing Polo

The Tang Dynasty
Height: 199 cm   Width: 154 cm
Unearthed in 1971 from Prince Zhanghuai's Tomb in Qianxian County, Shaanxi Province
   This scene was painted on the west wall of the tomb passage. Five players with mallets are galloping along the mountain valley to play polo. Trees and mountains are in the background. A very popular sport of the Tang Empire, polo was brought to China from ancient Persia. This painting is the earliest evidence of polo that has been found at the present time.

Watchtowers

The Tang Dynasty
Height: 280 cm   Width: 280 cm
Unearthed in 1971 from Prince Yide's Tomb in Qianxian County, Shaanxi Province
  On the east and west walls of the tomb passage there are pictures of watchtowers. This is the west piece. According to the Chinese traditional architectural principle, a large watchtower and two small watchtowers were arranged in the form of 'Three Watchtowers'.Behind them, there are trees and mountains. On the right, the low building that looks like a watchtower is the gate tower of the city.

Green-Glazed Pot with A Loop Handle and A Bottom In-Let

The Five Dynasties
Height: 18.3 cm   Diameter of Belly: 14.3 cm
Unearthed in 1968 from Binxian County, Shanxi Province

  This pot is in the shape of a ball. The simulated lid and the body are inseparable. On the handle is a phoenix whose mouth is in the shape of a mother lion feeding her baby. In the central bottom there is a small flower-like hole which is the only way that water can be poured in. It is a rare treasure of the Yaozhou Kiln.

Black Glazed Bowl with Oil-Drop Design

The Song Dynasty
Height:8.5 cm   Top Diameter:30 cm
Base Diameter:10.6 cm
Collected from Weinan City, Shaanxi Province
   This bowl was perfectly made and completely glazed except the bottom. There are some spots in the glaze which look like oil drops. Black glaze with spots is unique. It was popular in the Northern Song Dynasty, but it was diminishing by the end of the Yuan Dynasty. According to the features of the bowl, it is believed to have been produced in the North.

Shaanxi enjoys a reputation as the 'Homeland of Bronzes'. Since 1949, more than 4,000 pieces of bronze have been unearthed in the Province. Among our collection, the bronze wares are renowned for the wide range of sites from which they were unearthed, the large number of pit-store wares, large number of inscriptions and the important research value. For example:

a sword with a handle shaped like a horse's head, reflecting the style of the nomadic tribes in Northern China

a four-legged li unearthed in Southern Shaanxi

the 'Duo You ding', a tripod symbolizing the capital culture of the Western Zhou Dynasty

a sword embodying the development of metallurgy of the Qin Dynasty

These artifacts illustrate distinctive features of the times and regions that produced such ancient bronzes. From the Shang and Zhou Dynasties to the Qin and Han Dynasties, bronze ware changed its role from an object of ritual to an object for daily use.

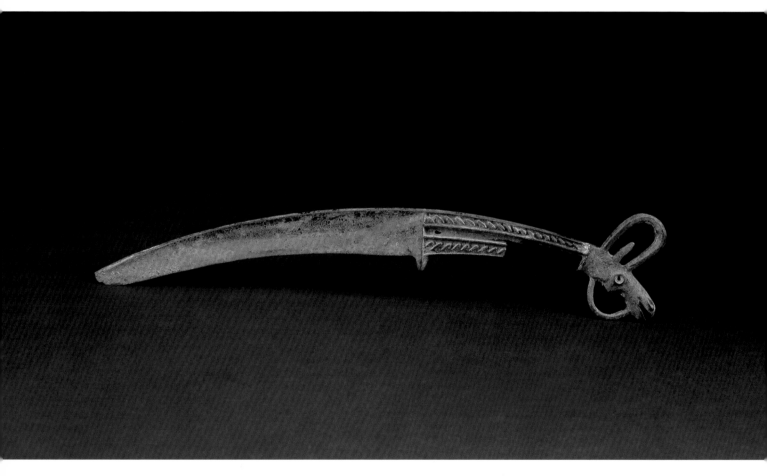

Sword with A Horse-Head-Shaped Handle

Late Period of the Shang Dynasty
Length: 32 cm
Unearthed in 1965 from Yantoucun, Suide County, Shaanxi Province

With a handle in the shape of a horse head, this sword is a gem of a collection of articles for daily use from a minority nationality of the Shang Dynasty, called 'Gui Fang'. This kind of artifact has also been excavated in Qinglong of Hebei Province, Shilou of Shanxi Province and Fuhao's Tomb of Yinxu Ruins at Anyang, Henan Province. Using the head of a snake, horse, or sheep as the handle of a knife or sword is the decorative feature of this nomadic tribe from Northern China.

Jue with Kui-Dragon Design

Late Period of the Shang Dynasty
Height: 20.3 cm   Length of Spout: 9 cm
Unearthed in 1965 at Yantoucun in Suide County, Shaanxi Province
    This is a wine vessel. Its features include a long spout, a deep belly,
and three high triangular legs, and it was decorated with a kui-dragon
design on its belly.

Ladle with A Sheep-Head-Shaped Handle

Late Period of the Shang Dynasty
Length: 28 cm
Unearthed in 1977 from Xiejiagou, Qingjian County, Shaanxi Province

This vessel for ladling out wine was crafted in a unique style. On its handle there is a tiger preparing to catch a sheep. The mould looks very vivid.

Four-Legged Li

Late Period of the Shang Dynasty
Height: 23.41 cm
Unearthed in 1981 from Longtouzhen, Chenggu
County, Shaanxi Province

This is a cooking vessel with four bag-shaped
legs. On its belly there is an ogre-mask design.
The unique mould makes it the only one among
the same wares in China.

Jia with Double Phoenix Pillars on Its Mouth

Late Period of the Shang Dynasty
Height: 41 cm   Diameter of Mouth: 19.5 cm
Unearthed in 1973 from Hejiacun, Qishan County, Shaanxi Province
    This wine vessel has a beast-head handle and three triangular legs with two phoenix-shaped pillars
on its mouth. On its belly there are two rings of ogre-mask designs.

Yue with Frog Design

Late Period of the Shang Dynasty
Length: 20 cm   Width of Blade: 15.7 cm
Unearthed in 1955 from Wulang Temple, Chenggu County, Shaanxi Province

    This object was used as a weapon or an instrument of torture. There is a hollowed-out frog in the center. The ware features the bronzes made in the Ba-Shu Area (also called Sichuan).

Man-Head-Shaped Mask

Late Period of the Shang Dynasty
Height: 16.5 cm   Width: 17.7 cm
Unearthed in 1976 from Sucun, Chenggu County, Shaanxi Province

This mask was used during the sacrificial ceremony. At that time, offering sacrifices to gods or ancestors was the most important national affair. Ancient people thought that wizards could connect with gods and communicate their intentions if they wore masks when they held the sacrificial ceremony.

Ox-Shaped Zun

Middle Period of the Western Zhou Dynasty
Height: 24 cm   Length: 38 cm   Depth of Belly: 10.7 cm
Unearthed in 1967 from Hejiacun, Qishan County, Shaanxi Province

   This wine container was made in the shape of an ox, with a square hole on its back and a tiger-shaped lid. The tail of the ox is the handle. The exaggerated mould is very magnificent.

Li Fang Yi, A Square Wine Container

Middle Period of the Western Zhou Dynasty
Height: 18 cm
Unearthed in 1955 from Licun, Meixian County,
Shaanxi Province

This wine container features a palace-roof-shaped lid, and it has two handles in the shape of an elephant's trunk. On the container and its lid is the same inscription, which has 10 lines and 108 characters. The meaning of this inscription is that a person named Li once wielded power, and as a historical material, it is valuable.

Meng Gui

Middle Period of the Western Zhou Dynasty
Height: 24.4 cm
Unearthed in 1961 from Zhangjiapo, Chang'an County, Shaanxi Province

As a food container, gui was usually used as a ceremonial object. On the inner base of Meng gui there is an inscription of 42 characters that tells the story of Meng's father, who followed Mao Gong to go out to battle and got a reward.

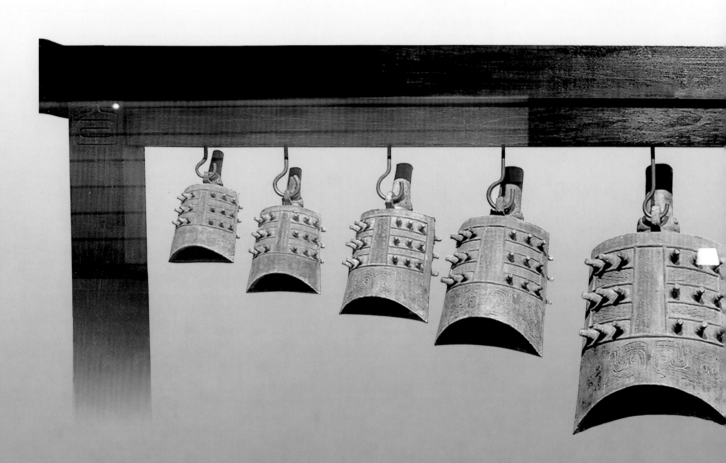

Zha Bells

Middle or Late Period of the Western Zhou Dynasty
Unearthed in 1960 from Qijiacun, Fufeng County,
Shaanxi Province

This musical instrument consists of 8 bells, graded
in size in order to produce the desired tone when struck
on the outside. Their bellies are decorated with kui-
dragon designs. The inscription records that Zha made
the bells to show gratitude to Master Zhong because he
had been given an award and appointed a post.

Wai Shu Ding, A Tripod

Middle or Late Period of the Western Zhou Dynasty
Height: 89.5 cm   Diameter of Mouth: 61.3 cm   Depth of Belly: 44 cm
Unearthed in 1952 from Dingtongjiacun, Qishan County, Shaanxi
Province

    The two ears of this tripod are decorated with tiger designs, and its
legs display the ogre-mask design. Inside it there is an inscription of
6 characters: 'Wai Shu Zuo Bao Zun Yi' .

Gourd-Shaped Pot with A Bird-Shaped Lid

The Warring States Period
Height: 37.5 cm
Collected in 1967 from Suide County, Shaanxi Province

The lid of this pot was made in the shape of a bird which was decorated with snake and bird designs on its chest. The pot was shaped like a gourd, with five bands and six interlaced hydra designs on its belly. The snake-shaped chain is connected to the hydra-head-shaped handle. It is a rare bronze gem.

Du Tiger-Shaped Tally

The Warring States Period (Qin)
Height: 4.4 cm   Length: 9.5 cm
Unearthed in 1957 from Duchengcun, Xi'an
   This tiger-shaped tally has an inscription of 40 characters indicating that the tally was the left tally controlled by a general who garrisoned in a place called Du. In ancient China, the tally was a token used by the king to control his army.

Sword

The Qin Dynasty
Length: 91.1 cm   Width of Blade: 3 cm
Unearthed in 1974 at the No.1 Pit of Qinshihuang's
Mausoleum, Lintong, Xi'an

This sword was made of an alloy consisting of bronze, tin and lead, etc.. Its surface was once treated by chromium, and for this reason it is still very bright and sharp even after being buried under the ground for 2,000 years.

Although the use of the gold and silver began early in China, it was still a luxury that only the upper classes could afford. However, in the Tang Dynasty, gold and silver wares were made and used in great quantity. Since 1949, more than 30 sets of gold and silver wares have been found in Shaanxi Province. In particular, a large number of Tang gold and silver has been unearthed; for example, in Hejiacun, Xi'an (1970) and Famen Temple, Fufung County (1987), causing quite a sensation. Such wares rank first in China not only in quantity but also in quality. The gold and silver of past dynasties collected here is very important in the research of manufacturing techniques and illustrating artistic features specific to the Tang Dynasty.

Gold Wood-Pecker, An Ornamental Object
The Spring and Autumn Period
Length: 1.5 cm   Height: 1.6 cm
Unearthed in 1986 at the No.1 Tomb of Qin Gong in the Fengxiang County, Shaanxi Province
   With big eyes and a high crest, this object was cast realistically.

Gold Monster

The Han Dynasty
Length: 11 cm   Height: 11.5 cm
Unearthed in 1957 from Gaotucun, Shenmu County, Shaanxi Province
  Standing on a lotus-shaped stand, the monster bends over to prepare to fight. It has a large horn which is divided into four branches and is decorated with a monster-head relief. Its tail is also decorated with a monster-head, and it rolls up and looks like a ring. Possibly it is an ornamental object of the Hun people who lived in the prairie in Northern China.

Gold Belt-Ornament with Double Camels Design

The Warring States Period or the Han Dynasty
Length: 7.6 cm   Width: 4 cm
Unearthed in 1974 in Longshoucun, Xi'an

On the back of this object, there are two semi-circular knobs. The center of the belt-ornament depicts a large tree with thick leaves and weeping branches. Beside it are two camels with branches in their mouths standing face to face. The design has a three-dimensional effect.

Octagonal-Petal Gilded Silver Cup with Musicians Design

The Tang Dynasty
Height: 6.6 cm   Diameter of Mouth: 7 cm
Unearthed in 1970 in Hejiacun, Xi'an

    The handle of this cup is formed by the heads of two Huns. On its belly, there were eight petals, and each was decorated with a Hun musician holding a musical instrument. The cup was cast into shape, and the decorations were engraved.

Gold Dragons in Running Position

The Tang Dynasty
Length: 4 cm   Height: 2.8 cm
Unearthed in 1970 from Hejiacun, Xi'an

These small dragons have two horns and a long tail and were decorated with fish scale patterns all over their bodies. They are exquisite artistic treasures of the handicrafts of the Tang Dynasty.

Octagonal-Petal Silver Cup with Hunting Scene and Ladies Pattern

The Tang Dynasty
Height: 5.1 cm   Diameter of Mouth: 9.14 cm
Unearthed in 1970 from Hejiacun, Xi'an

The patterns on its belly consist of two layers. The lower layer is a lotus petal design, while the upper depicts men hunting and ladies entertaining, dressing, playing with a baby etc.. The unique handle resembles a ring.

Six-Lobed Silver Plate with Bear Design

The Tang Dynasty
Height: 0.9 cm   Diameter of Mouth: 13.3 cm
Unearthed in 1970 from Hejiacun, Xi'an

This plate was hammered into shape. In the middle of it, a bear, which was covered with gold, is in growling position.

Silver Pot with Design of A Horse Dancing and Holding A Cup in Its Mouth

The Tang Dynasty
Height: 14.3 cm
Unearthed in 1970 from Hejiacun, Xi'an

This pot was made following the example of the leather canteen of the nomadic tribes. On the either side of it there is a horse design. The patterns confirm the historical account that Emperor Taizong trained fine horses which could dance accompanied by music. This artifact is a national treasure.

Silver Container with Flying-Lion Design

The Tang Dynasty
Diameter: 12.9 cm   Height: 5.6 cm
Unearthed in 1970 from Hejiacun, Xi'an
    The lid of this container was decorated with gilded
patterns of interlocking flowers and a lion in the center.
The vivid lion has two wings and is stepping on clouds.
On the container's base there are six rosette patterns
around the outside and a pomegranate in the center.

Gilt Silver Plate in Double-Peach Shape and with Double-Fox Design

The Tang Dynasty
Height: 14.5 cm
Unearthed in 1970 from Hejiacun, Xi'an

The unique shape of the plate is like a peach cut in half. There is one fox in the center of each half, and they are looking each other.

Silver Perfume Fumigator

The Tang Dynasty
Diameter: 4.5 cm
Unearthed in 1970 from Hejiacun, Xi'an

This object was made in the shape of a ball that was divided into two hollowed hemispheres with a pattern comprised of flowers, honeysuckle, grape and four birds. Inside the lower hemisphere there are two concentric rings and a small gold bowl. The bowl was used to burn incense and when linked with the rings, it could remain horizontal at all times and the condiment in it would not spill.

Silver Dish with Flowers Pattern

The Tang Dynasty
Height: 1.9 cm   Diameter of Mouth: 10 cm
Unearthed in 1987 from the Crypt of the Famen Temple, Fufeng County, Shaanxi Province

This tea dish was hammered into shape. Four round flowers are carved in the center of its inner base. The dish was used for the Royal Family to enshrine and worship the Buddhist's Finger Bone.

Silver Casket with Double-Phoenix Design

The Liao Dynasty
Height: 6.5 cm   Length: 7.2 cm   Width: 7.2 cm
Donated in October, 1993 by a French Connoisseur, Ms. Christian Deydier.

This casket's gilt design was hammered into shape. Each of the four sides of the box has a design with two flying phoenixes. On its lid there is a small rabbit design, and around it are interlocking passionflowers and honeysuckle patterns. On the inner base of the box an inscription of 24 characters was carved. Based on this inscription, the casket was regarded as a sacrificial ware of Prince Wenzhong, Han Derang.

Frescoes

The frescoes from the Tang tombs in Xi'an and surrounding areas in the Shaanxi History Museum amount to about 1,000 square metres. The social status of the deceased depicted include princesses, crown princes, nobles and high officials. The frescoes have a wide range of themes, including social life, etiquette, architecture and celestial bodies. Their painting styles took over from the Southern Dynasties and influenced the later Song and Yuan Dynasties. The Tang tomb frescoes make up an impressive picture depicting social style, especially that of the elite classes.

Guard of Honor in Procession

The Tang Dynasty
Height: 174 cm   Width: 216 cm
Unearthed in 1973 from LiShou's Tomb in Sanyuan County, Shaanxi Province
This scene was painted on the east wall of the tomb passage. The guard of honor consisted of 42 horses and 48 persons, so this is just a part of the whole painting. Some of the warriors wearing round-collar army uniforms hold red flags; some of them with swords wear red waistcoats. This is a valuable material for the study of the system of the guard of honor in the Tang Dynasty.

Maidservant Holding A Duster

The Tang Dynasty
Height: 145 cm
Unearthed in 1956 from Li Shuang's
Tomb in Yangtouzhen, Xi'an

This portrait is of a maidservant. She
has high-coiled hair, and wears a long
skirt, cloud-shaped shoes and a red shawl.
She holds a duster with her hands and
looks very respectful and submissive.

A Woman Musician Playing Xiao, A Chinese Musical Instrument

The Tang Dynasty
Height: 145 cm
Unearthed in 1956 from LiShuang's Tomb in Yangtouzhen, Chang'an County, Shaanxi Province

This scene was painted on the east wall of the tomb chamber. The painting depicts a woman musician wearing a man's costume --- a black turban, a red robe with a little bag hanging near the waist, striped trousers and white pointed shoes. She stands near the column and the crossbeam and is playing a Chinese traditional musical instrument called 'xiao'.

Maidservant Holding A Plate and A Jar

The Tang Dynasty
Height: 159 cm Width: 66 cm
Unearthed in 1976 from Princess Fangling's Tomb in Fuping County, Shaanxi Province

This portrait is painted on the east wall of the front tomb chamber. This maidservant's hair is styled in the traditional Hun fashion, and she wears Hun-style dress as well: a turndown collar, striped trousers and soft shoes. She holds a petal-shaped plate in her left hand and a jar in her right hand. Perhaps she is prepared to serve her master.

83

Dance and Music Performance

The Tang Dynasty
Height: 142 cm, 148 cm, 142 cm
Width: 141 cm, 137 cm, 141 cm
Unearthed in 1952 from Su Sixu's Tomb in the eastern suburbs of Xi'an

This scene of dance and music performance is painted on the east wall of the tomb chamber. In the center there is a Hun dancer with heavy eyebrows, an aquiline nose and sunken eyes. His dance is called the 'Hu Teng' Dance, and it came from the Western Area of China. To the left and the right there is an orchestra. This painting is valuable for the study of music and dance of the Tang Dynasty.

Palace Maids

The Tang Dynasty
Height: 176 cm   Width: 196.5 cm
Unearthed in 1960 from Princess Yongtai's Tomb in Qianxian County, Shaanxi Province

This famous painting is on the southern side of the east wall in the front tomb chamber. Nine palace maids carry a tray, a box, a candle, a round fan, a duster and a parcel etc. These maids have exposed necks, and six of them wear long skirts and shawls, while the other two girls wear man's dress. All of them look pretty, slim and graceful. The appropriate composition, smooth lines and proper color make this fresco one of the national treasures of China.

Hunting Procession

The Tang Dynasty
Height: 102 cm, 149.5 cm, 209 cm, 174.5 cm
Width: 117.5 cm, 185.5 cm, 162 cm, 220 cm
Unearthed in 1971 from Crown Prince Zhanghuai's Tomb in Qianxian County,
Shaanxi Province

   Against the background of hills and trees, more than 40 hunters appear in
the whole painting. Armed with bows and arrows, some of them carry flags,
whips, hawks and dogs. Some wear round-collared robes, and others wear
Hun-styled dress with a turndown collar. In the midst of so many attendants
riding around there sits a man with a calm expression riding on a white horse,
and he is probably the master of the tour. In the rear are two camels loaded
with their necessities. This magnificent work is the masterpiece of art in the
Tang Dynasty.

Receiving Foreign Guests

The Tang Dynasty
Height: 184 cm   Width: 243 cm
Unearthed in 1971 from Crown Prince Zhanghuai's Tomb in Qianxian County, Shaanxi Province

As a national treasure, this painting depicts the diplomatic affairs of the Tang Empire. The three persons with court dress on the left are Chinese protocol officials. The man to their right, bald with heavy eyebrows, sunken eyes and an aquiline nose, is the envoy from Eastern Rome. The man on the left, wearing the plume crown, is the envoy from Korea. The man on the far right is perhaps the minority nationality in northern China. This painting gives a true description of the friendly relations between the Tang Empire and the other countries.

90

Menservants with A hawk and A Dog

The Tang Dynasty
Height: 168 cm   Width: 133 cm
Unearthed in 1971 from Crown Prince Yide's Tomb in Qianxian County, Shaanxi Province

    Painted on the west wall of the 2rd corridor, the fresco shows that in the Tang Dynasty the nobles were fond of hunting. In the middle of the painting there is a tree and two menservants stand beside it. Both of them wear round-collar robes and black boots. The right one teases a yellow dog with a hunting hawk in his left hand. The dog wears a collar and is raising its head in response, with its left front claw on the man's thigh.

Palacemaids Holding Round Fans

The Tang Dynasty
Height: 129 cm Width: 166 cm
Unearthed in 1971 from Crown Prince Yide's Tomb of Qianxian County, Shaanxi Province

This scene was painted on the east wall of the third corridor. Two palace maids are standing beside a tree, each holding a round fan. Their hair is done up in buns, they wear long skirts and shawls, and their necks are exposed. Perhaps they are the female officials in the palace.

Pottery Figurines

As early as the 4th Century BC, earthen figurines were used in tombs within Shaanxi Province. From the Qin and Han Dynasties came the trend of burying the dead with luxurious honours and pottery figurines were used in large quantities as burial articles. The figurines were given definite features during the dynasties of the Qin, Han, Southern and Northern, Sui, Tang, Song, Yuan and Ming. Among them, those of the Qin, Han and Tang dynasties are the most exquisite: the strength and vitality of the Terra-cotta Warriors and Horses of the Qin Dynasty, the unadorned and delicate pottery figures of the Han Dynasty, the grand figures of the Tang Dynasty, the elegant and simple lines of the figures of the Song Dynasty. Such varying features show the Chinese tradition of sculpture in an incisive and vivid way.

Painted Pottery Figure Kneeling on Her Knees

The Western Han Dynasty
Height: 33 cm
Unearthed in 1966 from the satellite vault of Emperor Mother, Lady Dou's Mausoleum in Yangjiawan, Xianyang City, Shaanxi Province

This maidservant served the royal family. She wears three layers of robes and was painted with colors. It looks as if she is very faithful in the charge of her duties.

Painted Pottery Cavalryman

The Western Han Dynasty
Height: 69 cm Length: 55 cm
Unearthed in 1965 from Yangjiawan, Xianyang City, Shaanxi Province

    Grasping the halter in his left hand, this cavalryman wears a red robe with a piece of kerchief tied under his lower jaw. The horse reflects the features of the Wu Sun horse from the Western Area during the Han Dynasty.

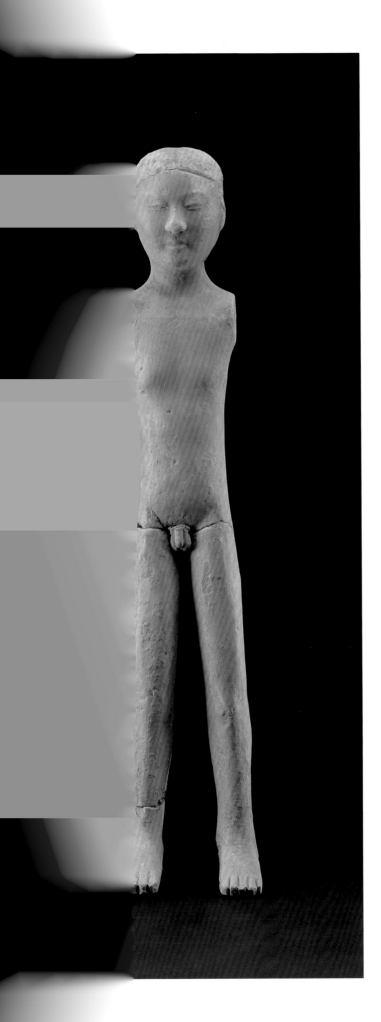

Painted Pottery Naked Man

The Western Han Dynasty
Height: 59 cm
Unearthed in 1959 near the Yangling
Mausoleum in Xianyang City, Shaanxi
Province

    This pottery figure was painted red. There
are two holes on his shoulder for attaching the
arms. The bottom of his left foot was engraved
with two characters 'You Che' which means he
is a soldier who drives the warchariot.

Pottery Figurine Blowing A Horn On Horseback

The Northern Wei Dynasty
Height: 39 cm   Length: 36 cm
Unearthed in 1953 from Caochangpo, Xi'an

    The horse wears a set of armour and the cavalryman is blowing a curved horn. Perhaps he is a bugler.

Pottery Figurine

The Southern Dynasties
Height: 29 cm
Unearthed in 1989 from Changling, Ankang City, Shaanxi Province

This man wears a cap and high boots, and he holds a drum-shaped object under his right arm. Perhaps there was once a drumstick in his left hand. His appearance is that of a Tu Fu who is in charge of sundry duties and protecting the manor.

Painted Pottery Woman

The Tang Dynasty
Height: 20.5 cm
Unearthed in 1972 from the
Zhangshigui's Tomb, Liquan
County, Shaanxi Province
    This woman wears a long skirt
and a scarf, and has snail-styled
hair. She looks very elegant.

Painted Pottery Woman in Hun Costume

The Tang Dynasty
Height: 50 cm
Unearthed in 1952 from Bianfangcun, Xianyang City, Shannxi Province

In the Tang Dynasty, the social atmosphere was very open. Wearing the Hun costume and wearing men's clothing was fashionable for a long time. This painted pottery woman is an example of that custom. On her body there is an inscription of two characters 'A Jian'.

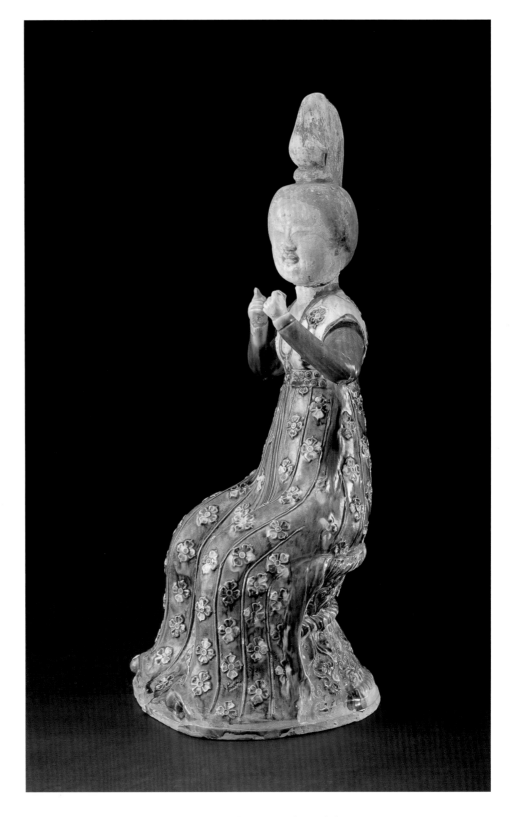

Tri-Colored Pottery Dressing and Making-Up Woman

The Tang Dynasty
Height: 47.5 cm
Unearthed in 1956 from Wangjiafen, Xi'an
 This woman has a high bun on her head, and she wears a beautiful long skirt and sits on a pier base. Perhaps there was originally a mirror in her left hand. This elegant woman is representative of the high Tang Dynasty.

Painted and Gold-Traced Civil Official

The Tang Dynasty
Height: 69 cm
Unearthed in 1971 from Zhenrentai's Tomb, Liquan County, Shaanxi Province
   The man looks very refined and veiled. He is a typical civil official of the
Tang Dynasty

Painted and Gold-Traced Officer

The Tang Dynasty
Height: 72 cm
Unearthed in 1971 from Zhengrentai's Tomb, Liquan
County, Shaanxi Province

Wearing a helmet and armour, this officer clenches his
fist and appears to have once held a weapon. He is very
awe-inspiring.

Painted Pottery Woman Holding A Mirror

850 AD(The Tang Dynasty)
Height: 30 cm
Unearthed in 1948 from Lady Pei's
Tomb in Chang'an County, Shaanxi
Province

This woman holds a mirror in
her right hand and wears a green
blouse and a grey white skirt. Her
full figure and decorous expression
manifest the aesthetics of Tang
people.

Painted Pottery Hun Person Fighting
With A Panther on Horseback

The Tang Dynasty
Height: 30.5 cm Length: 21 cm
Unearthed in 1960 from Princess Yongtai's Tomb in Qianxian County, Shaanxi Province
    This man wears typical Hun-styled dress with a turndown collar, and he has heavy eyebrows, sunken eyes and an aquiline nose. As he fights with a fierce panther, he looks very brave and robust.

Painted and Gilded Cavalryman

The Tang Dynasty
Height: 35 cm Length; 34.5 cm
Unearthed in 1971 from Crown Prince Yide's Tomb, Qianxian
County, Shaanxi Province

Sitting on the back of an armoured horse, this armoured cavalryman holds a weapon in his right hand and grasps the halter in his left hand. He was regarded as the guard for the procession of the crown prince.

Tri-Colored Pottery Hunting Figure on Horseback

The Tang Dynasty
Height: 36.2 cm   Length: 29.5 cm
Unearthed in 1971 from Crown Prince Yide's Tomb, Qianxian County, Shaanxi Province

   This cavalryman wears a robe with a round collar and appears to be shooting an arrow at something in the sky. The man and the horse were made with a skill called 'Jiao Tai' which means paste-mixing (two kinds of clay were mixed together), and it forms a kind of beautiful design, resembling a tree's annual rings. This pottery figure shows us that in the Tang Dynasty hunting was very fashionable.

Painted Pottery Musicians and Dancers

The Tang Dynasty
Height: 17.6 --- 26.2 cm
Unearthed in 1971 from Zhengrentai's Tomb, Liquan County, Shaanxi Province

    The seven pottery figurines are all girls. Of those seven, five are sitting musicians and two are dancers. During the Tang Dynasty, most of the officials liked music and dance. The set of pottery figurines may reflect the amusement of the owner of the tomb when he was alive.

Tri-Colored Figure Pulling A Horse

The Tang Dynasty
Height of Figure: 28.5 cm   Height of Horse: 40 cm
Length of Horse: 48cm
 Unearthed in 1959 from Zhongbucun, Xi'an
    Judging by his face, this man was likely a member of the Kun Lun
people who lived in other nations during the Tang Dynasty. These people
were taken from their homelands to the Tang Empire and served in the
noble families as servants.

White Glazed Man's Head

The Tang Dynasty
Height: 16.5 cm
Unearthed from Duan Boyang's Tomb at Hansenzhai, Xi'an, Shaanxi Province
 This is the typical image of a Hun person. With heavy eyebrows, big eyes and thick whiskers, the Hun man looks very vivid and funny. There are small broken crackles in the greenish white glaze. This piece is a gem of the Hun pottery figurines of the Tang Dynasty.

Painted Pottery 'Shuo Chang' Figures

The Tang Dynasty
Height: 18 --- 23 cm
Unearthed in 1966 from the western suburbs of Xi'an

'Shuo Chang' is a genre of popular entertainment consisting mainly of talking and singing. In the Tang Dynasty, it was a fashionable amusement. The two persons sitting on the base are musicians, and the standing old man looks as if he is talking or singing. The three figures are very vivid.

Pottery Dancer with Double -Rings-Styled Hair

The Tang Dynasty
Height: 37.8 cm
Unearthed from Guocun, Changwu
County, Shaanxi Province

This girl wears an exquisite outfit and has a slim figure and hair styled into double rings. Perhaps she is a dancer. This pottery figure is regarded as typical material for the study of the dancing and costume of the Tang Dynasty.

Pottery Figures Playing Polo

The Tang Dynasty
Height: 7.4 --- 12.8 cm
Unearthed from the Tang tomb in Guanshan, Lintong
County, Shaanxi Province

Polo, a kind of sport, came to China from ancient
Persia. In the Tang Dynasty it was very popular
among the noble society. The violence and thrill of
Polo even attracted most of the Tang emperors.

Painted Pottery Black Man

850 AD(The Tang Dynasty)
Height: 15 cm
Unearthed in 1948 from Lady Pei's Tomb in
Chang'an County, Shaanxi Province

This man has wavy hair, big eyes, thick lips
and black skin. During the Tang Dynasty, many
foreigners came into China by way of land or sea
on the Silk Road . Perhaps this man came from
Africa.

Maidservants Holding Goods

The Song Dynasty
Height: 34 cm
Unearthed in 1984 from Baijialiang, Ankang City,
Shaanxi Province

These four slim women respectively hold a
package for the musical instrument 'qin' , a painting
scroll, an inkslab and a book box.

Pottery and Porcelains

The invention of pottery is an important symbol of the Neolithic Age. Using clay, the ancient people produced pottery and so substantially improved their everyday life. Painted pottery is a mark of the Yangshao Culture. The appearance of porcelain began a new era in the history of Chinese pottery, which has lasted for some 8,000 years. From pottery came the primitive blue porcelain, and from blue porcelain came white porcelain. The Sui-Tang Period coined the phrase, 'The South is famous for Blue Porcelain, while the North is for White'. In Shaanxi, the wares of the Yaozhou Kiln are famous. After the Song Dynasty, elegant blue and white porcelain became typical. Underglaze red (you li hong), dou cai and famille rose decoration (fen cai) were also in vogue. The period of the Yuan, Ming and Qing Dynasties were the golden era for pottery and porcelain in China. The collections in our Museum help people to experience the charm of this ancient Chinese art.

Pottery Jar with Pointed Base

The Neolithic Age
Height: 43.8 cm   Diameter of Mouth: 6.2 cm
Unearthed in 1972 from the Jiangzhai Village Site, Lintong County, Shaanxi Province
   This water jar was made of red pottery. It has a small mouth and a slim neck with two rings on its belly for passing through a rope. There are carved string patterns on its upper belly. The jar is one of the representative objects of the Neolithic Age.

Painted Pottery Jar with A Slim Neck and Beast-Face Design

The Neolithic Age
Height: 27.5 cm   Diameter of Base: 8 cm
Unearthed in 1972 from the Jiangzhai Village Site, Lintong County, Shaanxi Province

　　The jar was made in the shape of a gourd. On the red background a black beast-face design was painted. The eyes look like crescent moons, and the noses are two round holes with a black spot in the center of each. On the beast's forehead there are lines. The jar is the rare work of the Yangshao Culture, and its painting is related to their primitive religion.

Reddish Brown Porcelain Zhong , A Container Ware

The Western Han Dynasty
Height: 44 cm   Diameter of Mouth: 17 cm   Diameter of Belly: 106 cm
Unearthed in 1962 in Xi'an
 This jar has two rings on the side of its large belly and it is decorated with three string designs. This porcelain object featured improved technology and was reddish brown glazed all over except the bottom.

White Glazed Bo with A High Stem

The Tang Dynasty
Height: 23 cm   Diameter of Mouth: 18.5 cm
Unearthed in 1956 from Duan Boyang's Tomb in Xi'an
    This object features a trumpet-shaped stem, and it has a design of printed strings, round and square flowers, and an engraved lotus pattern. The white glaze makes it very elegant. Among the white porcelain artifacts of the Tang Dynasty, it is rare to see the three technologies of printing, sticking and engraving used simultaneously in one object.

Tri-Colored Bowl

The Tang Dynasty
Height: 7.8 cm   Diameter of Mouth: 17.4 cm
Unearthed in 1960 from Princess Yongtai's Tomb, Qianxian County, Shaanxi
Province

The inner part of this pottery is hard and thin. A protruding string design decorates its belly. On its inner belly there are twelve green wide strings and some light brown lines. This bowl has a flared mouth and a short ring foot. In addition to the light yellow glaze, it was laid in green and brown colors. The elegant bowl is a perfect tri-colored ware.

Petaled White Porcelain Plate with A Character 'Guan'

The Tang Dynasty
Height:3.4 cm   Diameter of Mouth:13.5 cm
Excavated in 1985 from Huoshaobi, Xi'an, Shaanxi Province

The plate is in the shape of a flower with five petals. Because the fired pottery is hard, fine and thin, it is light in weight. Glazed all over, the plate is clean and white. There is a ring foot in which the character 'guan' is inscribed, meaning official. This piece was made in the Ding Kiln.

Petaled 'Mi Se' Porcelain Dish

The Tang Dynasty
Height: 4 cm   Diameter of Mouth: 24 cm   Diameter of Base: 14.5 cm
Unearthed in 1987 from the Crypt of the Famen Temple, Fufeng County, Shaanxi Province

This dish was made in the shape of five floral petals. It features a round mouth and a shallow belly, and its yellowish green glaze achieves the effect of jade. On its shoulder there are clear baked traces. This imperial ware was made in the Yue Kiln. It was called 'mi se' porcelain, which means 'the secret color' porcelain, because in the Tang Dynasty this kind of porcelain was only used by the royal family, and its glaze formula and burning technology were a secret to the public.

Greenish White Glazed Stem Cup in Shape of Six Petal Lotus

The Yuan Dynasty
Height: 7.9 cm   Diameter of Mouth: 8.3 cm
Unearthed in 1973 at Chunlin Village, Qujiangxiang in Xi'an

    These cups have a stick-shaped stem and look like a six-petal lotus. They have a greenish white glaze, and the inner part of the pottery was hard. This typical model of Yuan Dynasty wares was made in the Jingdezhen Kiln.

Brown Glazed Jar with Peacock and Peony Design in Gold Tracery

The Wanli Times of the Ming Dynasty (1573---1620 AD)
Height: 30 cm   Diameter of Mouth:5.9 cm   Diameter of Base: 8.8 cm
Unearthed in 1959 at Sigou in Yaoxian County, Shaanxi Province

    Between the neck and the belly of this jar there is a handle and a spout which are symmetrical. The knob of its lid is in the shape of a little beast squatting on its heels. Inside the jar was glazed in greenish white, while the outside has a gold design against the background of a brown glaze. On its base was written four Chinese characters 'Fu Gui Jia Qi' which means 'An excellent ware signifying wealth and honor'. It was made in the Guan Kiln in Jingdezhen.

Polychrome Ding with Ogre-Mask Design

The Ming Dynasty
Height: 12.9 cm   Size of Mouth: 12.9 x 12.8 cm
Unearthed in 1973 from Ma Longru's Tomb in Suide County, Shaanxi Province
    This piece was made in the shape of a rectangle with two ears and four legs. Its belly was decorated with an ogre-mask design, under which there was a square blue and white sign. This is a rare artistic work.

Soft Colored Insubstantial Porcelain Bowl

The Qing Dynasty
Height: 6.9 cm   Diameter of Mouth:13.2 cm
Collected in 1952 by the Former Shaanxi Provincial Museum

Insubstantial porcelain was a kind of porcelain with extreme thinness made by special technology. Its inner pottery is just like eggshells and is known for its thin and exquisite features. On both the outer and inner parts of the porcelain bowl are landscapes and portraiture designs. This Guan ware is from the Jingdezhen Kiln, and it has an inscription of four Chinese characters meaning 'Made in the Qianlong Times' on its base.

Bricks and Tile-Ends

In ancient China, many dynasties built their capitals in the Guanzhong Area (the middle part of Shaanxi). For this reason, a large number of palaces, official buildings, dwelling houses, temples, mausoleums and cemeteries were built in the region. Today, most of them have vanished but the architectural materials — bricks and tiles — can be found everywhere. Within the Museum we have pan tiles of the Western Zhou Dynasty, the imposing tile-ends from the Qinshihuang Mausoleum, the 'You Kong' tile-ends from Chang'an City (the capital of the Han Dynasty). Performing an important role in traditional Chinese architecture, such bricks and tiles help us understand more about building history and art.

Pan Tile with Double Tips

The Western Zhou Dynasty
Length: 46.2 cm   Width: 23.5 cm
Unearthed in 1976 from the Shaochen Site in Fufeng County, Shaanxi Province
On the back of this grey tile, there are slim cord patterns and double tips which could be used to link together. Pan tile was used on the ridge of a roof and the eaves during the Western Zhou Dynasty.

Tile-End with Deer Design

Qin State of the Warring States Period
Diameter: 14.4 cm
Unearthed in 1974 from the Yongcheng Site in Fengxiang County, Shaanxi Province

 The surface of this tile was decorated with a relief of a deer, which is jumping up and looks vigorous and elegant. It was one of the representative tile-ends of the Qin State during the Warring States Period.

Semi-Tile-End with Double Horses Design

Qin State of the Warring States Period
Height: 8.8 cm
Donated by Liu Baixun in 1956.

 In the middle of the tile there is a tree, and beside it, two flying gooses and two horses are face to face. The succinct tile-end shows the features of the Qi State during the Warring States Period.

Tile-End with Four Beasts Design

The Warring States Period
Diameter: 13.8 cm
Collected in 1984 in Fengxiang County, Shaanxi Province

The edge of the tile-end is protruding, and in the center four beasts are encircling a knob. The relief of the beasts looks vivid. This kind of design is rarely seen.

Tile-End with Panther Design

Qin State of the Warring States Period
Diameter: 14.5 cm   Width of Ring: 0.8 cm
Unearthed in 1956 in the northern suburbs of Xi'an

A string design decorated the edge of this tile-end. On its surface there is a relief of a very ferocious-looking panther that is turning its head and roaring.

Tile-End with Kui-Phoenix Design

The Qin Dynasty
Height: 48 cm   Diameter: 61 cm
Unearthed in 1977 from Qinshihuang's Mausoleum, Lintong County, Shaanxi
Province

In the shape of a semi-circle, this tile-end was used to cover the end of the
roof beams in large structures for decorating and protecting against decay. The
patterns on it are of the typical style of the bronze wares of the Shang and Zhou
Dynasties. Because of its large size, it was called 'King of Tile-Ends'.

Tile-End with Characters 'Yang Mang Wu Yin'

The Western Han Dynasty
Diameter: 18 cm
Collected in 1979 in Maoling Mausoleum of Xingping County, Shaanxi Province

A string decorated the edge of this tile-end. In its center there is a protruding
part, around which it was divided into four parts by double lines. Inside the four
parts four characters 'Yang Mang Wu Yin' compose an inscription meaning
'good luck'.

Green Dragon

White Tiger

Scarlet Bird

Xuan Wu

Tile-Ends of Four Direction Gods

The Han Dynasty
Diameter: 14.3 cm (Scarlet Bird)   13 cm (Xuan Wu)   19 cm (Green Dragon)
18.7 cm (White Tiger)
Collected in 1956 in the western suburbs of Xi'an

　　During the Han Dynasty, the Green dragon, white tiger, scarlet bird and xuan wu were called 'four direction gods'. They were used to prevent evil and symbolize the east, west, south and north. The set of four tile-ends were made similarly in composition. They were regarded as the finest works of the tile-ends from the Han Dynasty.

Tile-End with Characters 'You Kong'

The Western Han Dynasty
Diameter: 15.7 cm
Thickness: 2.5 cm
Unearthed in the Site of the Han capital Chang'an in Xi'an

With a wide edge, this tile-end was divided into three parts consisting of two outer parts with square designs and a middle part with an inscription 'You Kong', which means the tile was made for building an official (called 'You Si Kong') structure.

Tile-End with Characters 'Wan Sui'

The Western Han Dynasty
Diameter: 16.6 cm
Collected in the Site of Han capital Chang'an in Xi'an

This tile-end's inscription of two characters 'Wan Sui' was written in the seal script. It is a fine piece among the tile-ends of the Western Han Dynasty.

Decorated Brick with Receiving Guests Design

The Han Dynasty
Length: 47 cm   Width: 41.5 cm
Thickness: 5.6 cm
Donated in 1959 by the Sichuan Provincial Museum

This brick was made in a mould. In the center there is a watch tower symbolizing the great gate. Under the upper eaves there are two dancers on each side of the building. The person on the left side of the gate holds a 'jie' (a sign of the official), and the person on the right holds a shield. Perhaps they are the gate officials.

Square Brick with Lotus Design

The Tang Dynasty
Size: 32.5 × 34 cm
Unearthed in the Site of the Daming Palace in the northern suburbs of Xi'an

Made in a mould, this brick was decorated with a lotus design in the center and was used in the royal palace.

In ancient China, bronze mirrors were used as looking glasses when dressing and making-up. Most are round, some are in the shape of flower petals, others square. Some have handles. The viewing side is remarkably bright and the reverse is covered with decorative designs.. The elaborate casting techniques and varied patterning make the bronze mirrors not only practical but also beautiful works of art. In the developing history of Chinese bronze mirror design, there are three important stages: the Warring States Period, the Han Dynasty and the Tang Dynasty. Most of the Museum's collection dates from these three periods. The designs, casting techniques and inscriptions reflect the knowledge and artistic talent of the ancient peoples.

Bronze Mirror with Kui-Dragon and Curves Design

The Warring States Period
Diameter: 18.6 cm
Unearthed in Ansai County, Shaanxi Province

On the round knob base, the knob itself is not visible. Around the base are grass leaves designs, but the main patterns are four kui-dragons.

Bronze Mirror with Four Phoenixes and Curved Design

The Warring States Period
Diameter: 14 cm
Allocated by the former Northwestern Culture Department

This mirror features a three-stringed knob and a two-stringed knob base. It was decorated with four flying phoenixes against the background of cloud patterns.

Bronze Mirror with Four Circular Protrusions and Leaves Design

The Western Han Dynasty
Diameter: 18 cm
Donated in 1952 by Wu Yunqiao

This mirror has a knob base in the shape of 'shi di' ('shi' means persimmon, and 'di' means the base of the fruit). It also has an inscription of 12 characters 'Ri You Xi, Yi Jiu Shi, Chang Fu Gui, Le Wu Shi' , which means best wishes.

Bronze Mirror with Four Circular Protrusions and Four Coiled Serpents Design

The Western Han Dynasty
Diameter: 19 cm
Donated in 1956 by Wang Yaotang

Around its knob, there are twelve linking beads. Four circular protrusions, four coiled serpents, twelve birds and cloud patterns decorate the back of the mirror near its plain edge.

Bronze 'Shang Fang' Mirror

The Western Han Dynasty
Diameter: 16.3 cm
Unearthed in 1952 in Xi'an

The inside of the square frame is decorated with twelve 'di zhi' (Chinese ancient signs of indicating time). Outside of the square frame there are green dragon, white tiger, scarlet bird , xuan wu (a combination of a tortoise and a snake), birds, beasts and yu ren (people with wings), etc.. Near them is a circle of inscriptions which mean good luck. The two characters that begin the inscription are 'Shang Fang' , thus the origin of the mirror's name.

Bronze Mirror with Human,
Lucky Beast and Seal Patterns

The Three Kingdoms Period
Diameter: 15 cm
Unearthed in 1971 from Fucun in Zhangbagou, Xi'an

Around the knob base are patterns of human, lucky beasts, semi-circles and square seals. Near the edge there is a ring with an inscription of best wishes.

Bronze 'Ren Shou' Mirror with Four Direction Gods Patterns

The Sui Dynasty
Diameter: 25 cm
Unearthed in 1978 from Yongshou County, Shaanxi Province

This mirror has a ball-shaped knob, surrounded by decorations of the four direction gods, mysterious beasts, and Taoism immortals such as Dongwanggong (Royal Lord of the East) and Xiwangmu (Royal Lady of the West). Between two of the mirror's rings is an inscription. In addition, the twelve 'Sheng Xiao' (twelve animals representing the twelve Earthly Branches, used to symbolize the year in which a person is born), scarlet bird, xuan wu and flower patterns are on the back of the mirror.

**Bronze Mirror With Four Direction Gods
and Twelve 'Sheng Xiao' Patterns**

The Sui Dynasty
Diameter : 16.5 cm
Unearthed in 1952 in Xi'an

The Four Direction Gods (green dragon, white tiger,
scarlet bird and xuanwu) surround the round knob base.
Outside that pattern there are twelve 'Sheng Xiao' , and
every of them is in a frame. These decorations mean
good luck.

141

Bronze Mirror with Lucky Animal and Grape Patterns

The Tang Dynasty
Diameter: 10.9 cm
Allocated by the former Northwestern Culture Department
 This mirror has a beast-shaped knob and was decorated with grape and lucky animal patterns. Its decorations were regarded as one of the most attractive patterns of any mirror in the Tang Dynasty.

Bronze Mirror with Double Lions and Double Phoenixes Patterns

The Tang Dynasty
Diameter: 23.5 cm
Collected in 1952

In the shape of an eight-petaled flower, this mirror was decorated with a couple of phoenixes and lions flying in the grass. The phoenix and lion were common decorative subjects during the Tang Dynasty.

Bronze Mirror with Birds, Beasts and Landscape Patterns

The Tang Dynasty
Diameter: 20.2 cm
Unearthed in 1978 from Xuemeicun, Qianxian County, Shaanxi Province

This mirror has a bridge-shaped knob and a square knob base. Along the knob base there are four mountains with flowing water, flowers, grass, flying deer and birds beside them. It is a fine realistic landscape.

143

Bronze Mirror Showing A Legend
of Wang Ziqiao

The Tang Dynasty
Diameter: 12.9 cm
Unearthed in 1971 in Ankang City, Shaanxi Province

With a semi-ball-shaped knob, this mirror was made in the shape of the sun flower. Around the knob base, there are pictures of bamboo, a phoenix, a mountain and a man. It is said that Wang Ziqiao, a crown prince of King Zhoulingwang, also called Ji Jin, was skilled at playing 'sheng' (a reed pipe wind instrument). His music was like the chirping of a phoenix. The patterns on the mirror's back were cast according to this legend.

Bronze Mirror with the Eight Diagrams Design

The Tang Dynasty
Diameter: 16 cm
Unearthed in 1971 in Xi'an
This mirror has a knob in the shape of a tortoise, and the Eight Diagrams are around the knob. The Eight Diagrams were a common subject during the Tang Dynasty.

Bronze Mirror with Taoism Immortals Design

The Song Dynasty
Diameter: 20 cm
Collected in 1956 by the Shaanxi Provincial Museum
    This mirror was made in the shape of a petaled flower, with a bridge-shaped-knob in the center. Beside the knob there are two immortals of Taoism. The old one on the right is explaining the texts of Taoism, and the other one holding a plate is his servant. This scene reflects the atmosphere of idealism.

In Ancient China, jade was a favorite material. The ancients regarded jade as imbued with virtue and goodness and believed that such qualities could be passed on to the owner. In Shaanxi Province most of the ancient jade objects are unearthed wares. The Museum has a varied collection including:

a man's head of the Longshan culture from Shimao, Shenmu County in Northern Shaanxi

a parrot from the Fengji Tomb of the Zhou Dynasty in Fufeng County

the Empress' jade seal inscribed with the characters 'Huang Hou Zhi Xi' of the Western Han Dynasty from Lanjiagu, Xianyang City

several gold inlaid white jade bracelets of the Tang Dynasty from Hejiacun and Xi'an

Such pieces range from plain to elegant, realistic to abstract, unadorned to elaborate, yet all embody the styles of historic Shaanxi.

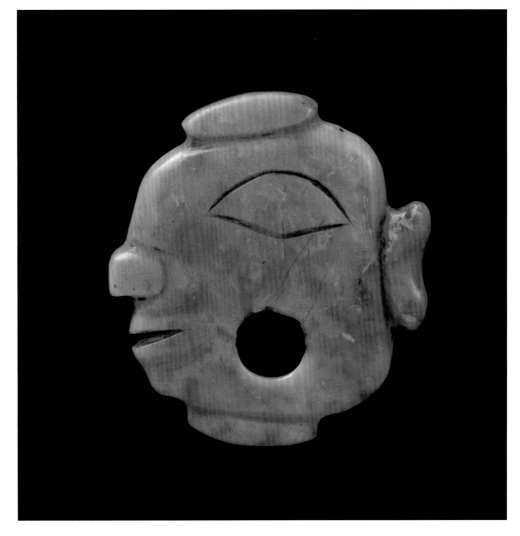

Jade Man-Head

The Neolithic Age
Height: 4.5 cm
Unearthed in 1976 from the Site of Longshan Culture in Shimao, Shenmu County, Shaanxi Province

This head has some brown stains from when the jade was buried beneath the earth. It was made in the shape of a flat piece. Plainly engraved on both sides, it has a hole for tying a rope on the man's face.

Jade Knife

The Neolithic Age
Length: 55 cm
Unearthed in 1976 from the Site of Longshan
Culture in Shimao, Shenmu County, Shaanxi
Province

    This rectangular knife was made of black
jade. The four holes in it are used to tie it to
other things. When used as a tool for cutting
grass, it was also called 'Shan Dao'.

Jade Cicada

The Western Zhou Dynasty
Length: 4.4 cm   Width: 2.2 cm   Thickness: 0.8 cm
Unearthed in 1974 from Zhuyuangou, Baoji City, Shaanxi Province
　　This jade ware is beige in color. The two small holes are used to tie a rope through the object.

Jade Parrot

The Western Zhou Dynasty
Length: 7.9 cm   Width: 4.9 cm
Unearthed in 1972 from Fengji's Tomb in Liujiacun, Fufeng County, Shaanxi Province
　　This flat piece was made of green jade and has two sides. One side is flat and the other is concave. Both sides were vividly and meticulously engraved with a parrot design.

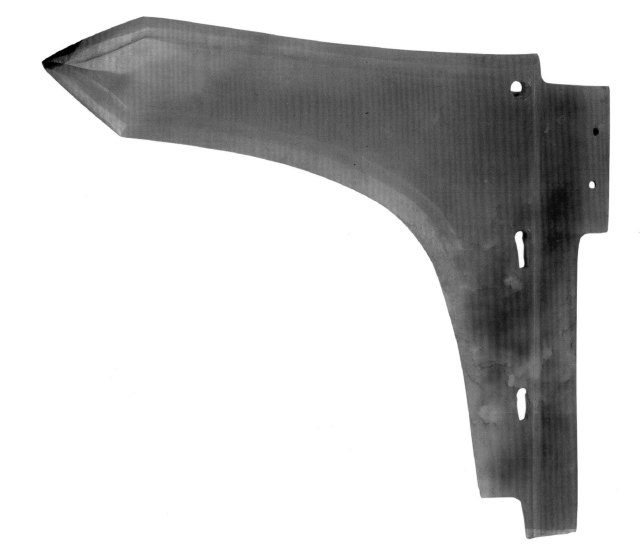

Jade Ge , A Weapon

Qin State of the Warring States Period
Length of Blade: 11.7 cm   Length of Na : 1 cm
Unearthed in1986 from Nanzhihuicun, Fengxiang County,
Shaanxi Province

This weapon was made following the example of the bronze wares. The holes were used for tying. At that time it was a ceremonial gift.

Jade Bi

The Western Han Dynasty
Outer Diameter: 17.4 cm   Inner Diameter: 2.8 cm
Thickness: 7 cm
Unearthed in Zhouzhi County, Shaanxi Province
    Bi , a round flat piece of jade with a hole in its center,
is a ritual object used for nobles offering sacrifices to
gods or ancestors, and holding funeral ceremonies. This
one is a typical object of the Han Dynasty.

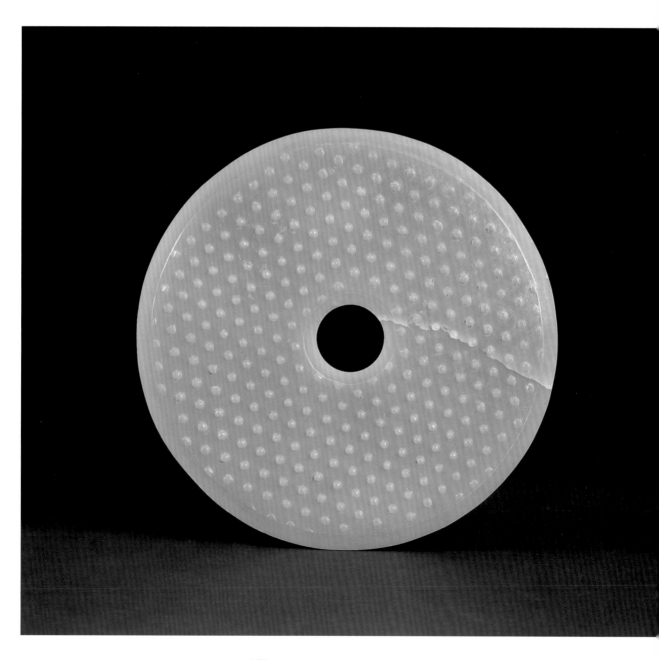

Gold-Inlaid White Jade Bracelets

The Tang Dynasty
Diameter: 7 cm
Unearthed in 1970 from Hejiacun in the Southern Suburbs of Xi'an

These bracelets were personal ornaments for the noble women in the Tang Dynasty. They were made of the Hetian Jade which comes from Xinjiang Uygur Autonomous Region.

Jade Belt Ornaments with Musicians Designs

The Tang Dynasty
Length of Side: 3.5 --- 4.5 cm
Unearthed in 1970 from Hejiacun in the Southern Suburbs of Xi'an

This set of ornaments consists of ten semi-elliptical objects, four square objects, one elongated-pointed-tablet-shaped object and one cha wei . On them are engraved designs of Hun musicians, playing musical instruments or dancing, full of vigor and vitality.

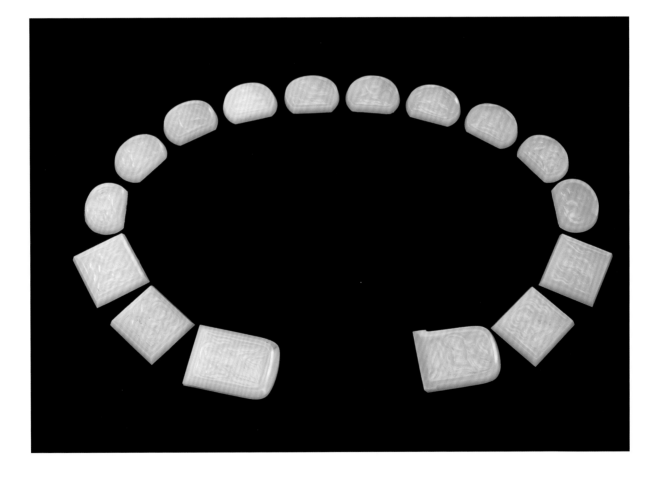

When direct exchange of goods gave way to using money, currency came in many guises. From the Spring and Autumn Period to the Warring States Period, shell coins were used rather than metal ones. In 336 BC, 'banliang' coins were cast in the Qin State. These coins were round in shape with a square hole cut out of the centre and established the basic form for ancient Chinese coins. In the Western Han Dynasty, 'wuzhu' coins symbolised the monopolisation of coin-casting by the central government. In the Tang Dynasty, 'tongbao' coins were decimalised and their names took on the new decimal system, rather than the traditional names given according to weight. From the Yuan to the Ming Dynasties, bronze coins were used instead of silver or paper money; the round coin with a square hole in its centre vanished until the Late Period of the Qing Dynasty. Shaanxi Province was responsible for the origins of the 'banliang', 'wuzhu' and 'tongbao' coins, as well as the starting point of the famous 'Silk Road.' With abundant ancient coins from home and abroad, our museum is an excellent place to enjoy and research ancient currency.

Knife-Shaped Money with Characters of 'Qi Fa Hua'

The Warring States Period
Length: 18.2 cm   Weight: 33 g
Collected in 1981

This piece was cast during the Qi State. Three characters 'Qi Fa Hua' were cast on its front side. 'Qi' refers to not only the Qi State but also to its capital Linzi City, now to the north of Linzi, Shandong Province. 'Fa Hua' means the standard money.

Money with Characters of 'An Yi Er Jin'

The Warring States Period
Height: 6.5 cm   Width of Shoulder: 3.7 cm
Weight: 32 g
Collected in 1972

    Cast in the Wei State, this money was circulated in the 'Three Jin' and 'Two Zhou' areas. 'An Yi' refers to the capital of the Wei State in the Early Period of the Warring States Period, now to the northwest of Xiaxian County in Shanxi Province. 'Jin' was a unit of money, and 'Er Jin' weights about 62.5g.

'Ban Liang' Coin of the Qin State

336 BC
Diameter : 3.1 cm   Weight: 5.4 g
Unearthed in 1962 from Shoupazhangbu, Chang'an County, Shaanxi Province

According to the large amount of Ban Liang coins unearthed from the sites and tombs of the Qin State in the Warring States Period, and according to the records of historical documents, it was ascertained that the casting of the Ban Liang coins began in 336 B.C.

Gold 'Wu Zhu' Coin

The Western Han Dynasty
Diameter: 2.6 cm   Weight: 9g
Unearthed in 1980 at Xianyang City, Shaanxi Province

The shape of this coin is the same as the bronze 'Wu Zhu' coins. On its front side there are two characters, 'Wu Zhu' , and a horizontal stroke. This is the earliest gold coin cast in the shape of a round piece with a square hole in its center that has been collected in our country.

Gold-Inlaid Money with Characters of 'Yi Dao Ping Wu Qian'

7 AD (Xinmang Period)
Length: 7.2 cm   Diameter of Head: 2.7 cm
Weight: 30g
Unearthed in 1965 from Liubucun, Xi'an

Two gold-inlaid characters, 'Yi Dao' , are on the round part of this coin beside the square hole. 'Ping Wu Qian' is inscribed on the long part of the coin. These five characters mean that this coin is equal to 5,000 Wu Zhu coins. It was cast for just two years and then its use was discontinued. This rare gem is the only gold-inlaid coin in the history of Chinese money.

'Yong Guang' Coin

465 AD (Song of the Southern Dynasties)
Diameter: 1.9 cm   Weight: 1g
Collected in 1996

This bronze coin, has two characters, 'Yong Guang', on its front side. Small and thin, this kind of coin was cast for only seven months and is rarely seen now.

Gold and Silver 'Kai Yuan Tong Bao' Coins

The Tang Dynasty
Diameter: 2.38 cm
Weight of Gold Coin: 6.9 g
Weight of Silver Coin: 5.3 g
Unearthed in 1970 from Hejiacun, Xi'an

The four characters on this coin, written by the famous calligrapher of the Tang Dynasty, Ouyang Xun, mean that it was the circulated money in the period of a newly established dynasty. At that time, gold and silver coins were used by the emperor to award nobles and officials and were not used for circulation.

Silver Persian Coin

590 AD --- 628 AD

Diameter: 3.1 cm

Unearthed in 1965 from the pagoda of Guoqing Temple in Tianziyu, Chang'an County, Shaanxi Province

Persia, today Iran, had frequent exchange of culture and economics with the ancient Tang Empire. This coin may have been delivered to China through the famous Silk Road .

Gold Eastern Rome Coin

610 AD---641 AD

Diameter: 2 cm   Weight: 4.6 cm

Unearthed in 1970 from Hejiacun, Xi'an

On its front side this coin has two kings' busts with crowns and armor. The left one is Heracilius in fighting robe, and the right one is his son. On the coin's back there is a cross and pedestal decoration around which is an inscription.

Japanese 'He Tong Kai Bao' Coin

710 AD
Diameter: 2.3 cm   Weight: 5.1 g
Unearthed in 1970 from Hejiacun, Xi'an

This silver coin was made during the Nara Period of Japan in imitation of the Chinese 'Kai Yuan Tong Bao' of the Tang Dynasty. Originally, both silver and bronze coins were issued, but the silver coins were abolished in the next year, and for this reason, the coin is a rare gem.

Bronze 'Gao Chang Ji Li' Coin

500 AD--- 640 AD
Diameter: 2.6 cm
Unearthed in 1970 form Hejiacun, Xi'an

Four characters, 'Gao Chang Ji Li', were cast on one side of this coin. Before the Tang Empire unified the Xinjiang Area, the Gao Chang Kingdom which was set up there cast this kind of coin.

Gold 'Chun Hua Yuan Bao' with Buddhism Statues Decoration

The Chunhua Period of the Northern Song Dynasty (990AD---995AD)
Diameter: 24 cm   Weight: 12 g
Unearthed in 1988 from Wutai Mountain, Shanxi Province

On the front side of this coin there is an inscription of four characters 'Chun Hua Yuan Bao'. On its back are two Buddhist statues, one sitting and the other standing on the lotus petals. Their five sense organs and costumes were engraved. This kind of coin was made by the royal family especially for the temples on Wutai Mountain during the Northern Song Dynasty.

159

The Museum houses many fine treasures; each exudes an air of mystery, with fascinating legends surrounding many of them, several conjuring up images of foreign cultures: the head-shaped bone carvings, many-faceted jet seals, a glass bowl with prominent ring decorations and a rare blue glass plate to name but a few.

Head-Shaped Bone Carving

The Neolithic Age
Height: 2.5 cm
Unearthed in 1982 from Hejiawan in Xixiang County, Shaanxi Province

This piece was made of animal bone. Its five sense organs are clearly shaped and the proportion is accurate. It is the earliest bone head-shaped carving found in our country.

Polyhedron-Jetted Seals

Western Wei Period of the Northern Dynasties
Height: 4.5 cm   Width: 4.35 cm   Weight: 7.57 cm
Unearthed in 1981 in Xunyi County, Shaanxi Province
   This 24-sided object was made of jet. Its 14 sides are individually inscribed with the different official titles of General Dugu Xin at different times in his life. It is the only seal which was made in this unique style.

Glass Bowl with Protruding Rings Decoration

The Tang Dynasty
Height: 9.8 cm   Diameter of Mouth: 14.1 cm
Unearthed in 1970 form Hejiacun, Xi'an
    This bowl was made of light yellow glass and is an imitation of Persian wares.

Blue Glass Plate

The Tang Dynasty
Height: 2.2.cm   Diameter of Mouth: 11.7 cm
Unearthed in 1987 from the Crypt in Famen Temple,
Fufeng County, Shaanxi Province

This light blue plate was an object for daily use,
originally made for the royal family during the Tang
Dynasty. Eventually it was awarded to the Famen
Temple. It is regarded as Islamic glassware from the
early period in ancient Western Asia.

Add:No.91,Xiao Zhai Dong Lu R., Xi'an, P.R.China
Z.C.:710061
Http://www.sxhm.com.
Tel:0086-29-5254727
Fax:0086-29-5262216

Editor-in-Chief:Feng Gengwu
Editor in Charge:Li Xiaojuan
Planned by:Su Donghui and Yan Xinzhi
Text by:Yan Xinzhi
Designed by:Wei Chunxue
Cover Designed by:Li Yunhui
Photographs Taken by:Qiu Ziyu
Translator:Bai Lisha
Proof-Read by:Keith Dede,Bethany Foland and Kate Astley
Made by: Shaanxi Xi'an Start Printing Co.

Shaanxi History Museum

Printed by Shenzhen Jinyu Printing Co.Ltd.
ISBN 7-5418-1671-X/J.404(0026800)